Report Writing Handbook

for the

Computer Forensic Examiner

Law Enforcement Edition

Bruce W. Pixley, CISSP, GCFA, EnCE

Author: Pixley, Bruce W.

Graphic design by Dennis Reneau.

Copyright © 2013.

ISBN: 978-1492208433

"If you cannot explain it simply,

you do not understand it well enough"

– Albert Einstein

Table of Contents

Acknowledgments

I want to thank God for all of the blessings He has provided in my life, especially my wife and daughters. I am grateful to my supportive family who has always encouraged me to help others with the talents He has given me.

I want to thank the Santa Barbara Sheriff's Department, especially Jim Thomas, Fred Olguin, and John McCammon. The department provided the foundation to start and pursue the field of computer forensics as a needed service to support all types of investigations. I was proud to be part of an agency that became a recognized leader in this field by providing instruction and assistance throughout the State of California.

I want to thank Thom Quinn who originally provided me with the opportunity and support to teach in this field. Since that time, I have been able to teach with some of the best instructors and meet students who have truly made a difference through their work.

I also want to thank all of the men and women in our great country who are serving or have served in uniform. May God protect you as you protect us.

About the Author

Bruce W. Pixley is currently operating his own computer forensics practice, Pixley Forensics Group. He has more than 25 years of combined experience in computer forensic analysis, high-tech investigations, and law enforcement.

He served 16 years as a sworn California peace officer and retired as a Lieutenant in the Santa Barbara Sheriff's Department. While working for the Santa Barbara Sheriff's Department, he was responsible for the creation and implementation of the county's first high-tech crime unit and computer forensics lab.

He has also been employed as a master instructor at Guidance Software. As an instructor, he developed course training materials and wrote manuals for computer forensic courses, such as Advanced Internet Examinations and Network Intrusion Investigations. These manuals were published by Guidance Software for use in its courses, which are taught to law enforcement and corporate investigators in the United States and foreign countries.

Since 2001, he has served as a lead instructor of computer forensics and network intrusion courses for the California Department of Justice's Advanced Training Center. As an instructor for both Guidance Software and the State of California, he has taught for over 2,000 hours on the subjects of computer forensics and high-tech investigations.

He possesses different professional certifications for his fields of work. These include the Certified Information Systems Security Professional (CISSP) certification and the GIAC Certified Forensic Analyst (GCFA), which are both ANSI ISO accredited credentials, and the EnCase Certified Examiner certification.

Since 2003, he has been retained as a computer forensic examiner and subject matter expert in both criminal and civil matters. He has been qualified as an expert witness in both state and federal court and testified about the foundation of computer forensics, Windows and Mac operating systems, chat software, Internet and network operations, e-mail, peer-to-peer file sharing, and Trojan viruses.

Foreword

When I joined law enforcement in 1989 and attended the police academy, part of the curriculum included report writing and courtroom testimony. We even had a few "mock" trials and discussions about courtroom demeanor, testimony and presenting your report. Even with that preparation, nothing really prepared me for what I faced once I was in the courtroom. The first year was a blur of learning just the basic etiquette and procedures, let alone trying to testify to specific facts. It was pretty overwhelming.

During that first year, I was astonished to see and hear of certain circumstances that precluded information from being presented, or when the information was presented, it was objected to on grounds that I had never heard of before. The surprising part for me initially was that the objection was not that the information was or was not true, but rather it was based on some type of procedural technicality that sometimes caused the information to be excluded from the case. I was shocked and confused.

A short time later, a very knowledgeable and seasoned Riverside County Deputy District Attorney named Martin "Marty" C. Brhel Jr. was handling one of my cases and sat down with me. It was the first time we had met and he wanted to just sit down and talk over the case to see how comfortable I was in the courtroom testifying. Sensing my frustration with some past cases, he told me a quick anecdote that has stuck with me to this day. Marty said, "A defense attorney is like a kid who wanders down the hall and ends up in front of a candy machine. Even though the kid has no money, he will push all the buttons in hopes that some candy will come out. Sometimes he will get lucky and something will come out, but often he will not." Marty went on to tell me that it was the defense attorney's responsibility to use all of the means available to help his or her client. That meant questioning my processes and procedures even when I knew they were done correctly and had the proper documentation to substantiate it. He also told me that if I didn't document something in a report, then it was as if it never happened. There would always be questions later if it was something significant as to why it was not documented.

From that day forward, throughout my entire law enforcement career, I always thought of that story every time I walked into a courtroom. The fact that no matter how much evidence or information may be present, the defense was going to always try and challenge it to try to make sure the proper process and procedures were followed and if not, have it excluded. It wasn't personal. It was just business and I needed to be prepared for it in my report and in my testimony.

Fast forward several years, and I had moved into a cyber-crime task force investigating all types of computer-related crimes. We handled many types of cases that involved newly adopted laws and dealing with documents in electronic form (emails, logs from ISP's, etc.) that had never really been presented in court before. It was like learning a whole new aspect of report writing and courtroom testimony over again, trying to educate the prosecutor and judges on technology and terms that were new and needed to be used to describe specific activity or circumstances.

Bruce Pixley

I first became aware of Bruce Pixley in the year 2000. At the time, the computer forensic community was much smaller than it is today and even smaller in the law enforcement community. Bruce was a Sergeant with the Santa Barbara Sheriff's Department and active in the cyber/forensic community. Even though we didn't meet until years later, I knew his name and his reputation for being a leader in the computer forensic industry. Bruce had become very active with California Department of Justice Advanced Training Center, which would offer computer forensic and high-tech classes to law enforcement personnel who were newly assigned to cyber-crime investigations and needed to learn about the tools, trends, and laws that were applicable.

A few years later, I was offered a job in the corporate sector with Guidance Software, which was a leading forensic training company and was producing one of the most popular tools used in law enforcement. I initially declined the job offer, but then learned that Bruce was joining their team. I reached out to him and we spoke several times by phone. Bruce had accepted the position with Guidance Software, but he remained neutral and offered me support in whatever decision I chose and encouraged me to follow my interests. I can honestly say that if it had not been for Bruce's support and the knowledge that we would have a chance to work together, I would not have left law enforcement and joined Guidance Software.

Once we both made the jump to Guidance Software in late 2003, we became instant friends. We both began working remotely on course development and researching all sorts of new technologies that could apply to computer forensics. We would talk daily about ideas and new things that we had found. Over the years that we have worked together, I have learned an immense amount from Bruce. He was always the one to push me farther and forced me to learn aspects of computer forensics that I had little interest. Many of the EnScripts I have written and released to the public were

due to Bruce constantly challenging me to build an EnScript based on some information or research that he had done.

Report Writing Handbook for the Computer Forensic Examiner

Finding computer forensic training today is not hard. Do a quick search on the Internet and you can find dozens of reputable training providers that offer comprehensive training courses in computer forensics. However, what almost all of those training courses lack is the final part (arguably the most important) of any investigation, the report writing and testimony of your findings.

It has often been said that you can do an amazing analysis job and find all sorts of very important computer forensic artifacts to support your case. However, if you cannot document those findings and be able to competently explain them in a manner which a non-technical person can understand, then you are missing the most important part of all your hard work (and research). Your work may be for nothing if it cannot be presented in court. This book provides that missing piece and important insight into report writing and courtroom testimony in a very specialized field. I only wished it had been available years ago to save me from some serious courtroom beatings. ;)

Congratulations to my friend and mentor on providing such a valuable book and resource!

Lance Mueller
Senior Incident Response/Forensic Analyst
IBM Emergency Response Services

Preface

I started my role as a computer forensic examiner in 1999. At the time, I was a Sheriff's Sergeant and I had been asked to assist in a case that the lead detective knew computers containing potential evidence were going to be seized during a search warrant. The lead detective asked a simple question: "Do you know how to handle computer evidence?" Digital evidence was foreign to us at that time. As I began to research the handling and analysis of digital evidence, I quickly realized that this was a specialty that required formal training and not something you could easily do on an ad-hoc basis.

During that same time period, law enforcement agencies in larger cities had started computer forensic labs years earlier and the smaller agencies were starting to ask that question more often. I then pitched the idea of our agency starting a high-tech crimes unit with a computer forensics lab.

My agency started the new unit with a sergeant, one detective, and a zero budget. Fortunately the Sheriff was very supportive and we were quickly funded to attend training and buy software. At that time, we started with EnCase 1.99L, which came on a 3½" floppy disk along with a serial port dongle and a thick grey mouse pad. For computer hardware, we started looking around the agency at what we could use or "borrow" from other units.

As anyone who starts a new unit knows, you begin to ask for help from other agencies as you are getting started. I recall my first phone calls were with someone who knew more than me and happily took my calls. His name was Bill Siebert and he worked for U.S. Customs. I remember that first phone call when he asked if I had "imaged" the suspect's hard drive. I had absolutely no clue what he was talking about. I am specifically taking the time to mention Bill's name because I was always grateful to him taking the time to help me. He took the time to help a stranger, provide some simple guidance, and to point me in the right direction. Since that time, I have always tried to pay it forward.

Of course, you can only do so much with information from phone calls. We began to attend the limited training classes that were available at the time. The California Department of Justice was an excellent resource for training and so was HTCIA. Our first HTCIA conference in San Diego was a real eye opener and I am grateful to the friends I met over the years through that association.

One of the challenges then (as it is today) was what information should we put into reports and how do we begin to explain our findings?

One of the observations I have had over the years is that new forensic examiners will often seek out other reports to get ideas of what should be included in a computer forensic report and how others have presented that information.

It seems like report writing has always been an issue for many forensic examiners. Some have been criticized if they put too much or too little information in a report. If you ask some examiners why they write in a specific format or include certain information in their report, you may get an answer like, "because … that is the way we have always done it around here."

As time went on, I became an instructor and taught for many years. I taught and worked with law enforcement and corporate examiners from around the world. I have worked with both criminal prosecutors and civil attorneys. I have also been called upon many times to testify in federal and state court to explain my findings to the judge and jury. For the forensic examiner, court testimony becomes the most important phase and the final culmination of his or her work.

Over the years, one of the things I have taken away from my meetings with the prosecution is that they do not understand the forensic reports that come across their desk. Along with not understanding the reports, they face the challenge of having to effectively present the information to the jury. I have often heard, "I do not understand what this forensic report says" and, "why do they write like that?" They are typically referring to a report that contains nothing more than bookmarked data and random notes from the Windows registry.

My goal in writing this handbook was to use my background, experience, and perspective to share how a computer forensic examiner can effectively communicate their findings to another investigator, the prosecutor, opposing counsel, and during trial.

Intended Audience

This handbook is intended to be the student manual in a formal law enforcement report writing class, which is geared for computer forensic examiners who are tasked with writing an expert witness report and may be called to testify in trial.

Organization of This Handbook

Section 1: Why Are We Here?

This section helps lay the foundation of expert witness report writing. It demonstrates the difference between electronic discovery productions and writing an expert forensic report. The forensic report not only contains the basics that should be in any report, but also the expert's opinions, which are based on factual objective findings.

Section 2: Starting Your Analysis

There are many ways to start the analysis and this section provides some structure to help quickly triage the analysis. By "walking the path," the examiner can quickly pick up on how a person used the computer, which provides direction for follow-up analysis. Use of virtual environment software, such as VMware, can be an extremely valuable aid during the analysis and for providing a demonstrative exhibit.

Section 3: Case Study

To help prepare for the report writing section, a sample case study is provided. This case walks through potentially relevant information that was discovered through the forensic analysis. Screenshots are used throughout the study to help provide a visual depiction and bring the case to life.

Section 4: Writing Your Report

A sample format of an expert witness report is provided as a roadmap to prepare the expert report. The report writing process is completed by using the information from the case study.

Section 5: Inside The Courtroom

At some point in the forensic examiner's career, the examiner may be called upon to testify in court. This section provides some helpful insight as to what to expect during a trial and the types of questions may be asked during cross-examination.

Appendix

Sample reports are provided as guides to offer examples for organizing and formatting your forensic reports.

Using VMware during your analysis can provide valuable insight to the way a suspect's computer was configured and used. As an aid, it can assist in providing screenshots for demonstrative exhibits. Step-by-step instructions are provided to boot the forensic image in a VMware machine.

Timeline analysis can help to connect other events and people behind the keyboard. This section includes information on how to setup and use the SANS Investigative Forensic Toolkit (SIFT) Workstation, mount an evidence file, and create a Super Timeline using log2timeline.

Find out how a demonstrative kiosk can provide a canned exhibit to provide the courtroom with an inside look of the user's computer.

Sample questions are provided as a guide for someone new to the interview process.

1

Why Are We Here?

I have reviewed many computer forensic reports over the years and most of them do not offer expert opinions. They have typically contained technical information, but not much of a narrative. Most reports are simple dumps of extracted information, bookmarked information, such as graphics, and sometimes volumes of superfluous information.

If you were to ask an examiner why specific superfluous information is included in their report, you will likely get the standard answer I mentioned in the preface: "Because that is the way we have always done it around here."

Certainly you may be employed by an organization that requires certain information to be included in every report. However, I would like you to look at the bigger picture and include information in your reports beyond that of what is just simply required. Start with the simple task of "how did the data get there."

Years ago, I recall a prosecutor calling me one day to discuss a case she inherited which involved a computer. Her words are very clear in my memory today: "I received an Encase report. What am I supposed to do with it?" The report she had listed hard drive geometry, a few bookmarked items, and no narrative.

This book is intended to show you the big picture of your work. From the time that you start you analysis, begin to think about how you may need to explain your findings to a jury. Since you may find yourself in the courtroom due to your role as a computer forensic examiner, this book gives you some insight on what you may encounter.

Electronic Discovery and Expert Witness Reports

If you were to take a critical look at most reports, you would find that they are not technically "expert witness" reports. Although the examiner who wrote it may even think or have been told that the report is an expert witness report, the reports are more like what I would refer to as a preliminary report. These types of reports would really be equated to an "electronic discovery" report or production.

Some of you may be wondering what is electronic discovery, also referred to as eDiscovery. You may have heard the term, but you're not quite versed on the definition. In the comparison below, I provide a simple definition of electronic discovery and provide some examples. I refer to one example as the "civil" version and the other as the "law enforcement" version (sometimes law enforcement sees their role as different as everyone else).

Civil Version of Electronic Discovery

Electronic discovery refers to the legal process in which there is an exchange of information between parties in an electronic format.

The potentially relevant data is identified, collected, preserved, processed (searched), and reviewed. The data, including metadata, is analyzed using digital forensic procedures and is often reviewed using a document review platform.

The review by counsel is to identify data for privilege and relevance before the production is turned over to opposing counsel.

Law Enforcement Version of Electronic Discovery

Typically, data is seized as evidence pursuant to a search warrant and preserved. The evidence is then analyzed and searched using digital forensic procedures based on the language described in the search warrant (looking for potentially relevant information).

Extracted data is then provided in a readable format for review by the case agent and prosecutor.

If the defendant is charged, the data is turned over to opposing counsel.

Difference?

What is the difference between these two examples? Both of these versions are similar in that the attorney or case agent is doing the review. However, what is not included in the scenarios above is no one is offering any opinions, such as when the information was stored, how it got there, if it ever was accessed or viewed, or if it was copied.

Those opinions are part of the role of the expert witness. It is those opinions that will begin to set apart an electronic discovery report from an expert witness report.

Sure, you may never know exactly who was behind the keyboard at a given time; unless, of course, it was captured by video. However, you may have objective findings from your analysis that will be helpful to the rest of the investigation.

The Basics of Report Writing

At some point in your career, you would have attended some type of report writing class. This handbook is not intended to replace that type of training. It is designed to expand on that training as it applies to your role as a computer forensic examiner and an expert witness.

In basic report writing, students are told that their report should answer the 5 W's (who, what, where, when, why) and the how. Why did some computer forensic reports stop answering these questions? Sure, the subject matter is technical and you may not be able to answer all of those topics, but the questions still need to be answered.

The problem with a lot of reports today is they are really just simple eDiscovery reports that only answer WHAT. Take a hard drive that contains 800 images of child pornography. The examiner bookmarks all of those images and attaches them to a report, which may read something like this:

> I conducted hash analysis of the suspect's hard drive and found matches for 800 images of suspected child pornography. I bookmarked the images and exported them to a compact disc for review by the case agent.
>
> No further action at this time.

The report simply explains WHAT and it may have moved the case off the examiner's workbench for a little bit. However, it fails to answer a lot of questions.

As you go down the list, how many of these additional questions could be answered?

WHO This may be difficult and you may not be able to answer this one. You did not witness the person behind the keyboard, but there may be other evidence, such as email or online banking, that could place a person behind the keyboard.

WHEN You may have thought you answered this by including the date and time stamps next to each image in your production of exported data. However, did you state the significance of the date and time stamps in your narrative? Or are you just assuming that everyone reading your report will know how to interpret that information?

WHERE Did you specifically tell the reader where the 800 images were located? Were the images all in one folder or in 3 different hidden folders within a specific user's profile? Was the data located in the user's Recycle Bin? Perhaps you included the full path next to the image, but do not identify the original folder that contained the files. It should not assumed that the reader knows how to interpret that information.

WHY You never want to speculate in your report. Unless the suspect tells you, you may never know why. However, files may be in a specific folder because that is where a program was configured to share or store downloaded files.

HOW Were all of the images located in the download folder associated with a peer-to-peer program? Again, never speculate. Just because they are in that folder, does that mean that the peer-to-peer program was used for downloading each of the images? You will likely need to provide some additional information and explain the different ways that the images were stored in that folder.

The Role of the Expert Witness

Based on your training, experience, and specialized knowledge of computer forensics (beyond that of an average person), you may be called upon as an expert witness. Rule 702 of the Federal Rules of Evidence defines testimony of an expert witness.

Rule 702. Testimony by Expert Witnesses

A witness who is qualified as an expert by knowledge, skill, experience, training, or education may testify in the form of an opinion or otherwise if:

(a) the expert's scientific, technical, or other specialized knowledge will help the trier of fact to understand the evidence or to determine a fact in issue;

(b) the testimony is based on sufficient facts or data;

(c) the testimony is the product of reliable principles and methods; and

(d) the expert has reliably applied the principles and methods to the facts of the case.

As an expert witness, your job is to prepare a well-written, objective report that contains your opinions and the supporting facts to support those opinions.

Some of you may have a difficult time in writing your opinions for a couple of reasons: 1) You lack enough training and experience to feel qualified to render an opinion; or, 2) You were told in your early training days that you do not write "opinions," you report the facts.

I can understand the person who feels that they lack enough training and experience to render an opinion. You should always feel confident about what you write. In fact, I believe that confidence is one of the strongest traits you can possess. If you have to present information to the jury, you should be confident.

If you are withholding your opinions because you are only supposed to report the facts, I want you to take a look at a simple law enforcement scenario:

> At 1:15 am, an officer stops a car for swerving over the double yellow lines three times within a quarter of a mile. The officer smells alcohol coming from the driver's mouth. The driver has red blood-shot eyes and his speech is slurred. The driver admits to drinking two beers at a local tavern.
>
> The officer conducts some field sobriety tests with the driver, such as horizontal gaze nystagmus test, walk and turn test, and one-leg stand test. The driver also submits to a field breathalyzer, which displayed a reading of .18 percent.
>
> Based on the officer's formal training and experience, along with his observations, driver's statement, and the objective symptoms of intoxication observed during the field sobriety tests, the officer arrests the driver for suspicion of driving under the influence of alcohol.
>
> About one hour later, the driver submits to a breathalyzer at the police jail facility, which displayed a reading of .17 percent.
>
> The officer writes this information in a report.

In this scenario, would you consider the officer an expert witness? The officer's report contains facts, but it also contains opinions. The opinions are based on his objective findings.

The same holds true for a computer forensics examiner and his expert witness report. The opinions are not based on wild guesses, they are based on objective findings and supporting facts to support those opinions.

Fact or Opinion?

During training, you were likely told that your investigation needs to only contain facts. Facts can be proven. On the opposite side of facts, are opinions. Simple opinions can be based on guesses, speculation, and gut feelings. Do not include simple opinions in your report.

Just remember that there is a difference between an "opinion" and an "expert opinion." The expert opinion is based on a combination of experience, training, and education. The expert opinion is also supported by objective findings and based in fact.

Review the following opinion statement:

> The 32 digital images of child pornography were likely downloaded using LimeWire peer-to-peer software because they were all located in a folder called Shared.

Would you consider the statement to be an opinion or an expert opinion? Without any other information to support that statement, it would fall into the category of a simple opinion. The word "likely" also diminishes the statement.

If you are a law enforcement officer and your case is going to trial, the prosecution will be looking for an expert report and an expert to present digital evidence in court. Your role as an expert witness is to educate the jury. If you are confident and have command of the facts, you will be able to easily communicate with the jury.

Let's look at the previous statement again, but this time it is written as an expert witness opinion:

> Based on the date and time analysis of the files and the recovered download records, the 32 digital images depicting child pornography located in the Shared folder were downloaded from the Internet using LimeWire peer-to-peer software between November 3, 2011 and November 5, 2011

Trial Experience

Some of the best experience you will ever have in your career will be trial experience. However, many cases are closed by a person accepting a plea bargain or some other type of settlement. This affects computer forensic examiners because their reports and analysis is never challenged by an opposing side. The examiner also does not get the opportunity to explain the findings in court.

While you may have experience testifying in court, testifying as an expert witness is different. Your trial experience may be limited to your observations at a crime scene or testifying to statements made by a suspect during a short interview at the crime scene. In this scenario, you end up with: "I came. I saw. I heard. I left."

As an expert witness, you will be asked to report your findings and teach the jury the meaning and significance of those findings. For some people, your findings could be very complicated. However, your job is to explain it as simply as possible.

While it is important for you to understand the technical aspect of computer forensics, do not feel like you have to prove how smart you are by your technical explanation to the jury. If you think you are going to get the jury to understand what happened by explaining there are 8 bits in a byte, 512 bytes in a sector, and how many total sectors there were on a particular hard drive, you are mistaken. Leave your propeller cap in the lab and do not "geek out."

Report Writing and Rule 26

As I mentioned earlier, some examiners do not know where to start when writing an expert witness report. The Federal courts have standards that need to be followed. If your report contains information that supports these standards, you will always be on solid ground.

This type of report is referred to as a Rule 26 Report. The name is derived from the Federal Rules Civil Procedure, Section 26(a)(2)(B). This standard calls for the following:

A. Written report that is signed

1. Complete statement of all opinions

2. Complete statement of the basis and reasons for all the expert's opinions

3. Exhibits to be used as support for or a summary of the opinions

B. Qualifications

C. List of all other cases in which the expert has testified at trial or at deposition in past 4 years

D. Publications in the past 10 years

E. Compensation for review and testimony

I want you to be aware of Rule 26, especially if someone ever asks you to write a Rule 26 report. For the purpose of this handbook, I am going to focus on the first section listed above (written report that is signed), which describes your written report.

Target Your Audience

As you write your report, remember that your report needs to have two focal points: 1) Reader comprehension; and, 2) Rule 26 guidelines. Now that you are aware of Rule 26, it's time to focus on reader comprehension.

I have reviewed reports that were written in a way that no one other than someone with a strong background in computer forensics would understand. While the reports may have been technically accurate, most readers (especially the target audience) would not understand it. I have also reviewed completed reports that were no more than a bookmark report from Encase or FTK.

I have often been asked how a report should be written. The simple answer is "tell the reader a story." Complete the picture by using your knowledge and expertise to provide the background to the facts you found. For example, in a non-fiction novel, an author will introduce a character or event by providing a description along with a background and history to tie everything together. Your report should be the same. If you find an important piece of evidence on the hard drive, state why it is important, how it got there, and how it may relate to other evidence.

Think of it this way, if I were to put you in a room with people who have very little computer experience, how would you explain it to them? Ultimately that is what you will be doing if you have to appear in court. If a reader, such as a prosecutor, cannot understand the words in your report, how will the jury understand what you are telling them? Based on your writing, will the prosecutor be confident that you can explain it to the jury?

Remember what I said earlier about confidence (that word will come up again). As you write your report, write with confidence and state things clearly (also known as keep it simple).

By now in your career, you are probably aware that a reader will judge you based on your writing skill. When you pause to think about it, who will be reading your report?

- Supervisor
- Peers
- Investigators
- Management
- Prosecutor
- Opposing counsel
- Opposing expert witness

The people reading your report are making decisions and your expert report can easily become the determining factor in a case. If you write poorly, it may be perceived that you lack skills as an examiner or that you are someone who would not be a good witness if brought into court. Conversely, a defendant may plead out prior to trial due to your well-written report. The defense will read all of the facts you intend to testify to in trial and see the best option is to take a plea agreement.

As you are writing your report, you need to remember that the reader may be looking to you to establish the corpus or elements of a crime. If so, does your report contain that information?

For example, a person carrying a backpack with a laptop that has 800 images of child pornography may be facing a charge of possession of child pornography. Your report contains basic information and you bookmarked all of the images. However, did you check to determine how the images were stored on the hard drive? Were they downloaded from the Internet? Or were the photographs taken by the suspect using a camera seized in his possession during his arrest? What started out as a possession case, may actually be a case involving receipt or production or even distribution. Of course, you will need to present those elements in your report.

Objectiveness

As you write, make sure that you use objective language and do not add subjective characterizations. If you remember that you goal is to write an objective report, then it will be easy to use objective language.

You never want to give the reader the feeling that you are biased in your report writing or that you included any speculation. If you were to start a statement with "It is very clear…," what facts would you have to support that statement?

Statement Using Objective Language

A computer user downloaded 11 known digital images depicting child pornography from the Internet using Limewire peer-to-peer software between November 3, 2011 and November 5, 2011.

Statement Using Subjective Language

Based on the volume of child pornography downloaded from the Internet by the suspect, it is very clear that he, like most pedophiles, was only seeking to build his personal collection of child pornography.

When you are objective in your analysis and report writing, you will look at the big picture and see things that others may not see. Here is a simple 5 paragraph example of a case that objectivity will help to demonstrate how the computer is being used:

① A search warrant was conducted based on a peer-to-peer (P2P) investigation. During the initial investigation, an IP address was identified as a distribution point for a couple of movies that depicted child pornography.

② A person was identified based on subscriber information associated with the IP address and a search warrant was obtained for his residence. His computer was seized and I was asked to conduct a forensic analysis of the hard drive.

③ During the analysis, I confirmed that the computer that was seized was the same computer that was the subject of the initial P2P investigation.

④ His hard drive and his external hard drives contained over one hundred thousand digital images and movies of adult pornography.

⑤ After reviewing his collection of images and movies, I found one single digital movie that depicted child pornography. The movie had been downloaded 9 months prior to the time his computer was seized. However, I could not find any evidence of him downloading other child pornography or even viewing that specific

movie. In fact, the analysis indicated that it had never been viewed since the time the download was completed. This movie was downloaded when hundreds of other movies were being downloaded during that same week.

Remember to be objective during your analysis because a report with limited or excluded information could easily affect decision-makers who read it. What type of decision might be made if the following occurred?

1) Paragraph 4 was excluded?

2) Paragraph 5 only stated: "I found a digital movie that contained child pornography. The movie had been downloaded 9 months prior to the time his computer was seized"

Hedge Your Bets

When writing your report, you need to use precise and confident language. You do not want to give the impression that you are unsure of the facts or your expert opinion. A simple way to demonstrate your lack of confidence is by using hedge words. These words are red flags that demonstrate a noncommittal to a statement and make you sound equivocal.

Here is a simple list of hedge words and phrases that should be avoided:

- might be
- could be
- may
- seems to be
- appears to be
- possible
- believe
- think
- suggests
- implies
- sometimes
- usually
- perhaps

Review the following three statements for the use of hedge words:

1) *"Based on the current state of these documents, it appears there has been continued use and access of this data by the defendant."*

2) *"Based on the evidence, I think the user deleted several folders containing digital photographs."*

3) *"It appears the defendant's computer was running peer-to-peer software, which could have been used to download digital movies that depicted child pornography from other computers on the Internet."*

How could these statements be rewritten by using more confident language?

When you proofread your report, eliminate the hedge words and ensure your report contains objective findings that support the statements. You never want to give the impression that you are being speculative and you are likely mistaken.

In contrast to hedge words, you should avoid words that characterize something as absolute, such as ***never*** or ***always***. For example, if you were trying to explain file creation time stamps and you wrote something to the effect of "the file creation time stamps *always* means …"

The Nail Approach

A problem with some reports is when the author tries to apply a "cookie cutter" approach to every single report. As most seasoned examiners already know, you cannot have just one forensic tool in your toolbox to get the job done. As the saying goes, if your toolbox only contained a hammer, then everything becomes a nail. Report writing can follow the same logic and not all reports can be a nail.

The following two scenarios contain some sample questions that you should consider answering when conducting your analysis and writing your report. These questions are not meant to be an exhaustive list of every question you should try to answer. Just remember, a simple guide for your report will be to answer the 5 W's and the how.

Child Exploitation

When you find images or videos depicting child exploitation, try to answer the following questions:

1) How and where did the files get stored on the hard drive?

2) Who has access to these files?

3) When were the files stored?

4) What other activity was occurring at the time? Can you associate that activity with a specific person?

5) Did someone view the files? If you can confirm the files were viewed, when and which software was used?

6) Were the files backed up to external media, optical media, or online storage?

7) Were the files shared or distributed to anyone else?

You may not be able to answer every question, but the answers to most of these questions will help to paint a picture for the reader to understand. You may also have hundreds or thousands of images and videos and trying to answer these questions for every single file could be a huge task. As a general guide, I suggest that you provide the reader with a history of at least 10 files.

Check Fraud

If you have a case involving check fraud, try to answer the following questions:

1) If checks were found on the hard drive, how did they get there? Were they scanned or was software used to generate them?

2) Where were the files stored and who had access to them?

3) When were the files stored?

4) How often was the software used?

5) What scanner or printer was used?

6) What other activity was occurring at the time the checks were created? Can you associate that activity with a specific person?

Technical Terms

If you need to include any technical terms, you will want to include the definition for the reader. This can be accomplished in a footnote or within the same paragraph that you first mention the term. Some writers may include definitions in a separate section; however, they need to point the reader to that section. Never assume that the reader will know to flip to the last page or an appendix to find a laundry list of definitions.

Boilerplate Language

You need to be careful about using any boilerplate language that may not be appropriate. This can often happen when someone uses a report written by someone else as a starting point. This boilerplate language may not be applicable and you may not even understand the relationship of it. You could easily find yourself answering a lengthy series of questions during trial that you are not prepared to handle. If you look around the office for boilerplate language, I am sure you will find examples that should not be used.

> "...conducted a search of the computers and computer system components, such as the central processing unit (CPU), ..."

> Really? You actually searched the CPU?

Recap

In this section, I have drawn the distinction between the types of forensic reports that may be generated. When a forensic examiner is asked to conduct an initial analysis of digital media, the examiner may produce a preliminary report, which is a type of electronic discovery production. This type of report can be quick to generate and very helpful for key people involved in the early stages of an investigation.

However, as an investigation continues, a prosecutor may request more in-depth analysis and an expert report. This handbook covers how to prepare an expert report and prepare for trial.

Writing Tips

1) Tell the reader a story.

2) Write with confidence and state things clearly.

3) Try to answer the 5 W's and the How.

4) A reader is making decisions and will judge you based on your writing skill.

5) If the reader cannot understand what you are writing, how will a jury understand it?

6) Use objective language. Do not add subjective characterizations.

7) Avoid bias and speculation in the report.

8) Define all technical terms and abbreviations.

9) Be careful about using any boilerplate language that may not be appropriate.

10) Do not use simple opinions.

2

Starting Your Analysis

As you conduct your forensic analysis to prepare your report, you are likely to conduct some sort of triage to help you see how the computer was being used.

In the past, I have heard students ask for a checklist of items they should review in every case. I personally do not use a checklist as each case is different and may require some thinking outside of the box. A checklist may cause a person to focus too much on a cookie-cutter approach to computer forensics. This is demonstrated in the case study in the next section.

I prefer to start with an understanding of the case. I may obtain that through the initial reports that are available or a search warrant affidavit. Affidavits are very helpful since someone had to explain it to a judge for authorization and they are likely to contain key relevant pieces of information. Plus, if you are conducting an analysis based on a search warrant, you will want to read the entire search warrant so you are aware of the scope or limits of your analysis.

As you approach your analysis, look at the hard drive the same way as a detective may examine a crime scene at a house. Each room is a little different. Some evidence is obvious, such as blood stains or broken glass, and some evidence is not visible with a simple glance.

One of the most challenging perspectives a new forensic examiner has is by looking at digital evidence through forensic software. Certainly the obvious such as digital photos in the user's My Photos directory are easy to find. However, forensic software today provides an overwhelming amount of information. I cringe when I see

someone process three 2TB hard drives by indexing all of the drives along with selecting every script or process their forensic software will allow. When it is finished (if it finishes without crashing multiple times), they look like a deer staring into headlights trying to figure out where to start.

Observation

Your analysis will likely be limited in scope based on the search warrant issued by the judge. However, if you were not limited, would you be able to examine every single detail of the hard drive and include every observation in your report? Not likely. Honestly speaking, you will not have enough time to devote to that type of exercise.

If someone does not understand the volume of data, it may be necessary to explain it in terms that people can understand:

One megabyte of storage space is the equivalent to a single book containing 500 double-spaced pages of text. A single gigabyte of storage space, or 1,000 megabytes, is the equivalent of 1,000 books. A hard drive capable of storing 160 gigabytes would be equivalent of 160,000 500-page books.

Do you have time to study every page of 160,000 books and put that information into a report?

A new detective learns that the successful way to track a suspect and solve a crime is to try and walk the same path. By walking that path, the detective studies the environment and hopes to pick up clues along the way that help to solve the crime.

As you head down the path, remember that you have been tasked as an objective fact finder. You are also looking for exculpatory evidence. It is very possible that the subject of your investigation did not commit the acts for which he is being accused. If you find that type of information, you will want to disclose it because you never want to be accused of concealing information. Your integrity is very important and if you lose it, well, let's just say it will be time for you to do something else.

Walk the Path

As opposed to doing what I would refer to as "new guy forensics[†]," here are my tips to help you triage your evidence and "walk the path." This high-level approach will help you easily spot the clues that require additional attention. This section is not meant to be an exhaustive list of everything you could look at, but it is a start. Of course, do not forget the basic techniques you were trained on, such as hash and signature analysis and keywords, to help guide your analysis.

One of the first things I like to do as I start my analysis is prepare the suspect's hard drive to run in a virtual environment, such as VMware. Prior to using VMware, I used to restore the suspect's image to a new hard drive, thus creating a working copy that could be installed in the suspect's computer. I prefer taking 15 to 20 minutes to get the image running in VMware than waiting for an image to restore. Plus, VMware lets me establish snapshots so I can easily go back to a specific point in my analysis. As you view the evidence through VMware in one monitor, you can look at the actual evidence loaded in your forensic software in a second monitor. Additional information about VMware is located later in this section.

When you sit down at the suspect's computer, you want to see what he saw. Did he have to use a password to login? What did his desktop look like? Were all of his contraband images and videos stored in a couple of folders on his desktop? Not only does this review help the examiner, some simple screenshots will also help the jury understand what was going on as well. Do you think the jury would rather see screenshots of the suspect's computer environment or screenshots of forensic software sorted three different ways and a complex explanation of what they are seeing?

Operating System

During your analysis, you will quickly want to identify the operating system and version. As we have watched versions of Windows change, we learned that each generation has differences that you need to consider. For example, is it Windows XP or Windows 7? How does the operating system impact last access time stamps? Some other questions to consider are as follows:

[†] New Guy Forensics defined: Switch to gallery view, page-down, page-down, page-down, bookmark, page-down, page-down, bookmark, etc.

- What accounts were active? Is it a multi-user setup or did everyone in the house use a single login?
- Were the accounts password-protected?
- Is there archived data in the Volume Shadow Copy? How are you going to extract that data?
- What activity was going on with the user's Recycle Bin?
- Did the user try to hide data by simply setting the folder attribute to hidden?

Personal Documents

Are there personal documents stored on the hard drive, such as Microsoft Word? Who are they associated with and what is the date/time activity of those files? These documents are a great way to demonstrate ownership.

You will also want to look for personal journals, letters, photographs, resumes, tax documents, and work-related documents.

Email Client/Web-Based Email

Does the person use an email client to download their email, such as Microsoft Mail or Outlook? Or does the person use a web-based email account?

Times have changed and there are less remnants of web-based email on the hard drive compared to 8 years ago. However, it is still worth a look. Even if you cannot recover the body of a message, you can hopefully determine the person's email address or recover a listing of the email in their inbox.

You will want to look through email stored by an email client for communication that will help to demonstrate ownership. The attachments on sent and received emails may also provide relevant information to your investigation.

Don't forget that sent email may be used to help tie a specific person to the computer at a specific time.

Password-Protected and Encrypted Files

You will want to look for password-protected files, such as Zip or RAR. Likewise, you will want to look for encrypted data. It is a simple place for someone to conceal their

data from other users. Some people also compress multiple files because they are uploading their data to the Internet to share with other people.

If password-protected files do exist, the next challenge is for you to break the password. Always start by looking for the low hanging fruit to break them. People are lazy and may have stored their passwords in a simple text file. You may also find them in the registry or associated with Internet browsers. Here is a simple scenario addressing how passwords may help your investigation:

> A Windows 7 computer is used by three people in a house. Each account, including one used by the suspect, is password-protected. You also find ten Zip files that are password-protected and are associated with the suspect's user account. Based on the filenames within the Zip files, they appear to contain child pornography.
>
> In less than an hour, you are able to break all three user login passwords and each one is different. The password used by the suspect happens to open each Zip file and you confirm they do contain child pornography.

Needless to say, this information should go in your report.

Chat Logs

Get in the habit of looking for chat logs. While some chat programs may not be configured to record conversation, some people like to maintain their chat logs. If they exist, the logs may be used to demonstrate the user's intent or M.O.

Internet History

When the person surfs the Internet, which browser does he or she use? You may focus all of your attention on Internet Explorer and find nothing. Do not forget to look at browsers such as Firefox, Chrome, Opera, or even something outdated such as Netscape.

Once you determine the browser being used, what sites does the person visit? Are there any sites that requires a login? What search engine was being used and what types of searches were being conducted?

In one well-known case, the defendant was conducting his online banking at the credit union, which required a username and password to access the account. At the same time, the defendant was downloading child pornography and sending email messages regarding his eBay transactions. The jury put a lot of weight into this activity as it tied a specific person to the keyboard.

Just be aware that the way browsers handle Internet history can be complicated, specifically with date and time stamps. A lot of high-profile cases have involved a defendant's Internet history. If you have to testify, you will want to be confident in your findings.

Installed Programs

You will want to look at the types of programs a user had installed. The installed programs will help to give you a sense of how the computer is used.

Does the user have 5 or 6 different digital photograph and digital video programs? You will want to look at each one to determine if these programs store a listing of recently-accessed files.

Does the user have newsgroup software installed? That may indicate their desire to download and upload files. Or perhaps the user subscribes to a newsgroup service, but he prefers to use the web-based interface.

Along with installed programs, look at the history of the programs. What files have been recently accessed and when?

While I have recommended that you should use a virtual environment to conduct your analysis, you will always want to check to see if the person you are investigating was using one as well. You could find your analysis having little or no results because all of the activity is located inside of a virtual hard drive. If you see a virtual environment program installed, start looking for virtual hard drive files. You will need to export these files and analyze them separately.

External Storage Devices

Do not forget to look for external storage devices. Most people do not want to lose their data (their collection of "stuff"). They are very likely to back it up. Is it backed up on a 2TB USB drive or cloud storage?

A quick check for external storage is look at the Windows shortcuts (.LNK files). Do you see any association with an external drive letter? However, a more thorough check will be for you to look at the Windows registry and log files.

Hopefully, all of the external drives were seized and are part of your analysis. With the drives in your possession, what else is stored on the device? Date and time analysis will help you determine activity and some personal files may help to show ownership.

If you have a USB device, make sure you check the embedded USB serial number of the device. This serial number may match up to the registry, which can help you tie the device to the computer and possibly the user.

Malware Detection

The subject of malware detection is more in-depth than what this handbook is geared for; however, it is something that you will want to consider during your analysis. Especially since the Trojan virus defense may be raised at some point.

First off, you will want to check for anti-virus/malware software installed on the hard drive. If it was installed, was it active and were the definitions up to date? If you run the computer in a virtual environment, you will have an easier time in looking for these answers through the user interface. If it exists, look at the logs and see if anything had ever been quarantined or deleted.

Another step will be to use your version of anti-virus software to scan the hard drive for viruses. You can either use the anti-virus software on your forensic computer to scan it or you can use a pre-built virtual machine with anti-virus software installed. The latter approach allows you to use one or more virtual machines with a different anti-virus program installed on each one.

While you may not possess the skill set to conduct follow-up analysis if a virus is detected, you will want to make note of it in your report. Conversely, if no virus is detected, make sure that is in your report as well.

Cause and Denial

Now that I have covered malware and the possibility of a Trojan virus defense, it is time to consider other causes or denial that may be claimed as a rebuttal to your findings. Sure, you may have found illegal content on the defendant's hard drive, but

that is only the beginning. Taking the time to consider these types of scenarios will help you maintain your objectivity as their claim may be true.

This section is not meant to be an exhaustive list of possible defenses, but it is a starting point. Here is a short list for you to consider along with suggestions for follow-up analysis:

Bulk Download

This is a defense used in peer-to-peer cases when the defendant downloaded files in bulk by selecting every file listed in the search results pane. The defendant may claim that his intent was to search for legal adult pornography, selected every file in the results pane, and then clicked the download button. He was then shocked to learn that some of the files that were downloaded depicted child pornography. Consider these questions during your analysis:

1) Do the date and time stamps of the downloaded files indicate that they were downloaded at the same time? Instead of only listing the child pornography in your report, you might want to consider listing all downloaded files along with file created and last written date and time stamps.

2) Could you recover the user's search terms?

3) Can you recover filenames from the file that is used to track downloads in progress? This data may still be resident in the unallocated space of the hard drive. In one case, I was able to recover the filenames of over 2,000 files that were either downloaded or attempted to be downloaded. That type of listing may be a good demonstrative exhibit.

SOD Did It

This is where the defendant claimed that the acts were committed by SOD (some other dude). This other person could be someone else who lives in the house or Ray the homeless guy who visits the house every now and then. Consider the following:

1) Did the computer have multiple user accounts and were they password-protected?

2) Is there any indication that different people used the same user account? This could be based on personal documents or Internet-related activity. Look for activity that may be user-specific, such as online banking or email.

3) Interview other people in this house to determine if, how, and when they used the same computer. Did they only log into their account and never used the defendant's account? Did they know the password for the defendant's account?

Never Looked

If child pornography is found, the defendant may claim that if it existed, he never knew it was there and never looked at it. Consider the following:

1) Look for evidence of viewing the files. This may be in the form of Windows LNK files, index.dat records, Windows registry, or a file-viewing program that tracks recently viewed files.

2) Were the files moved from one folder to another folder (such as the default downloads folder to a folder called Saved Movies)?

I Deleted It

A defendant may claim that he deleted the illegal content once he discovered the offensive content on his computer. Consider the following:

1) Are the files located in the user's Recycle Bin?

2) Did the user backup the files prior to deleting them? Look for evidence of the files being stored on removable media.

3) If you only find images in a thumbnail cache file, look for the original files. They may have been deleted or they may have been backed up prior to deletion.

4) Does the defendant use any type of encryption, such as TrueCrypt or PGP? The files may have been moved into an encrypted container to conceal them.

The Interviews

As you have seen from the last section, the possible defense of someone else did it may be used. A good interview can help to minimize this type of defense, especially when it is not disclosed until a year later and a month prior to trial.

If you were not directly involved with the interviews, it would be a good idea to read the reports or listen to the audio recordings of the interviews of people who used the digital evidence. The information gathered from these interviews will help to provide some guidance during your analysis. The interviews are also a great way to tie down someone's story on their use and association with the digital evidence you will be analyzing.

During the interview, the suspect may make statements regarding how he used his computer in conducting criminal acts. For example, the suspect may admit to using a specific screen name and email account to send and receive child pornography. During your analysis, you would be looking for information to either corroborate his statements or show he was providing false information.

What if you found the computer had two or more accounts? Did the suspect say anything about how each person had a separate account? How did the suspect keep his activity hidden from the other users? Did other people have access to his account? These are only a sample of questions that should be asked.

If you are not directly involved in the interviews, the person conducting the interviews may need some assistance with the types of questions to ask. Categories of questions and sample questions are listed in Appendix E of this handbook. These questions are meant to be a simple guide to provide some direction. The person conducting the interview should try to ask open ended questions to elicit responses beyond yes and no, such as "Tell me about your background with computers."

VMware Analysis

When I first started conducting computer forensic analysis, I would often come across potentially relevant findings that I would not understand. The finding may have been based on the results of a keyword search or just finding an installed application that I have never used before. For example, a keyword search hits on the words "preteen" and "PTHC" in some little unknown data file.

Ultimately I knew that when I wrote my report, I would need to explain the finding to the reader. If I just bookmarked the finding and included a snippet of text or binary data in my report, the reader would come back to me later and ask, "what is that?" Sure, it would be easy to tell them, "well, I was hoping you would know." Of course that does not fly, especially when you are the "computer guy" and everyone assumes that you know everything.

In order to conduct some follow-up analysis of how a program may function, I had two options: 1) Restore the image of the suspect's hard drive to a new hard drive and place it in the suspect's computer; or, 2) Install the same operating system and program on a new hard drive and place it in a lab computer. After running some tests, I would then extract the new hard drive and examine it for any changes that may have occurred. Both of these options were very time consuming.

Another option was to read any research or informational papers my peers may have written on the subject. However, I ultimately knew that I would be the person who would be called to testify on my findings. If you are challenged during a trial with how do you know something to be true, you want something a little more than, "I read a paper posted on a message board on the Internet; therefore, it must be true."

My research methodology changed when I was introduced to VMware (Figure 2-1). I first learned about the benefits of using VMware from one of my co-instructors back in 2002. This software provided a huge value in the lab as it saved me time and resources. I could easily test operating systems and programs without having to dedicate an entire lab computer to the process. Within a few years of that time, forensic examiners started trying to figure out ways to run VMware using a forensic image as the virtual hard drive. That was not a large leap since VMware already handled dd images.

As I continued teaching, I would often make comments in the classroom about the benefits of VMware in the lab. Students began to request formal training and I eventually added it as a block of instruction to the forensic courses I was teaching.

Another great addition to my analysis toolbox was being able to import a VMDK file (VMware virtual hard disk) to my forensic software for analysis. This allowed me to conduct analysis in a controlled environment within VMware and then import the VMDK file into my forensic software for analysis to determine exactly what changes occurred or artifacts could be found. I used this same environment when I was teaching network intrusion courses.

Figure 2-1 – Using VMware to test software in a controlled virtual environment

I encourage all examiners to continue reading papers written by their peers on new subjects. The next step is for them to validate that information by conducting analysis in a controlled environment that is similar to the computer being investigated. For example, if you know a little about a specific peer-to-peer program, you may be confronted with a different version. Using VMware will allow you to test the software to find the answers to questions such as:

1) Are the user's search terms stored?[‡]

[‡] This brings us back to the unknown data file that you found during a keyword search as it contained the words "preteen" and "PTHC." During the VMware analysis, you learn that the file was actually part of a peer-to-peer program. Those terms were the user's last search terms and appeared in a dropdown menu in the user interface. You create a screenshot as a demonstrative exhibit and attach it to your report.

2) Where are user settings stored?

3) How are temporary files created when a file is being downloaded?

3) How does the software track downloaded files in progress?

4) What happens to a file when the download is complete?

5) How does the software affect date and time stamps, such as file created and last written times?

Conducting this type of analysis to understand how things work not only makes you a better examiner, it will also make you feel more confident if called to testify in court. Your methodology to conduct your analysis was in a controlled environment, which allowed you to document the processes and it is also repeatable. If another examiner conducted the analysis using the same environment and methodology, would the results be the same?

If you are new to VMware, start out by building a simple machine running your favorite operating system. Beyond that, Appendix B of this handbook provides you with a step-by-step method to use a forensic image as the virtual hard drive in a VMware environment.

Timeline Analysis

As you conduct your examination and find relevant files, you should consider the following types of questions to add context to your findings:

1) How did the file get there?

2) Have the files ever been accessed?

3) What other activity was occurring around that time?

4) Can a specific person be associated with the computer at that time?

For example, if you were conducting an examination to search for child pornography, finding that type of material may be a very simple exercise. You find the illegal content and bookmark 62 digital photographs and 11 digital movies depicting child pornography. These bookmarks would note the date and time stamps along with the folders the data was stored in.

At this point, some new examiners may feel that their job is finished and they are ready to move on to the next case. This reminds me of the new patrol officer in the field: "I came. I saw. I arrested. 10-8."

Depending on what you were tasked to do, that may be true. However, in some instances, this is just the starting point.

Based on your initial analysis, let's assume (for the moment) that you suspect this content was downloaded from the Internet. Now you need to prepare for the real challenge. Starting with one of the digital movies, answer the following questions:

1) How was it downloaded? What program was used?

2) When was this movie downloaded? Are you able to determine when the download started and when it completed?

3) Are you able to determine who downloaded the file? Can you put someone behind the keyboard?

4) What other activity was occurring on the computer during the time of this file being downloaded?

5) Can you find any evidence of the movie being played?

6) Was there any effort to save or backup the file after it was downloaded? Was the file originally downloaded into one folder and then moved into another folder?

To answer some of these questions, timeline analysis will take an active role in your investigation and make this task much easier.

To conduct timeline analysis, start with the "event" itself. The event may be a file saved on the hard drive, an email message being sent, a chat conversation, or some other type of significant finding in your investigation. Once you have an event identified, you will want to look at what else was occurring before and after the time of that event.

So, how do you start the timeline analysis? First, you need to know that there are two types of timeline analysis. One is referred to as "file system timeline analysis" and the other is often referred to as the "Super Timeline."

The first method, file system timeline analysis, is based on file system metadata. If the partition of the hard drive was formatted as NTFS, then the metadata

would contain the following time stamps: creation, modified, MFT record modified, and accessed. As a new examiner, you would focus on this type of timeline analysis.

File system timeline analysis is a fast and easy approach. However, while this may sound simple, it may still be challenging for a new examiner as he has to have a good understanding of each time stamp.

At the start of a case, I will often generate a file system timeline that I can easily review in Excel. This way, if I find something of interest (an event), I can quickly look at the spreadsheet to see what else was occurring before and after the event.

The Super Timeline analysis is much more complex and granular. It is based on pulling time stamps from the file system metadata plus operating system artifacts and program artifacts. The operating system artifacts, such as Windows shortcuts, Recycle Bin activity, Prefetch files, event logs, and the registry hives (to name a few) all contain time stamps. Compound this with program artifacts that contain time stamps, such as browser activity. This type of analysis is much more in-depth and requires experience in understanding the artifacts and how to interpret them.

Do not feel that because file system timeline analysis is fast or simple, it may be inferior to the Super Timeline approach. The latter approach takes significant time to create and may easily generate millions of records.

A framework that was created to generate a Super Timeline is called log2timeline, which was created by Kristinn Gudjonsson. If you wanted to get started in using this program, it is already configured and ready to go by using the SANS Investigative Forensic Toolkit (SIFT) Workstation.

The SIFT Workstation is a free download created by the SANS Institute. It is a VMware machine built on the Ubuntu operating system. Whether you are working with a segmented Encase evidence file (.E01) or a dd image, there are tools within this preconfigured workstation that will mount the image. Appendix C provides an introduction on how to use the workstation and log2timeline.

At a high level, the process of using log2timeline for timeline analysis is as follows: Extract all of the date and time stamps and put them into a single CSV file, which is referred to as a bodyfile. Once you have collected the time stamps from the file system metadata and various events, you will want to filter that data down. This filtering is designed to handle tasks such as removing the duplicates and applying a date range filter.

Once you have a filtered CSV file, you would import that file into Excel. Once this data is in Excel, you will want to apply a couple of actions, such as sort, filter, and freeze the top row. A sample is provided below.

A	B	D	F	K
date	time	MACB	sourcetype	desc
5/23/2010	22:59:40	...B	NTFS $MFT	/Users/Owner/Documents/My Received Files/09.jpg
5/23/2010	22:59:41	.A..	NTFS $MFT	/Users/Owner/Documents/My Received Files/09.jpg
5/23/2010	22:59:42	M...	NTFS $MFT	/Users/Owner/Documents/My Received Files/09.jpg
5/23/2010	23:05:05	...B	NTFS $MFT	/Users/Owner/Documents/My Received Files/08.jpg
5/23/2010	23:05:12	.A..	NTFS $MFT	/Users/Owner/Documents/My Received Files/08.jpg
5/23/2010	23:05:18	M...	NTFS $MFT	/Users/Owner/Documents/My Received Files/08.jpg
5/23/2010	23:09:32	...B	NTFS $MFT	/Users/Owner/Documents/My Received Files/012.jpg
5/23/2010	23:09:33	MA..	NTFS $MFT	/Users/Owner/Documents/My Received Files/012.jpg

Figure 2-2 – Sample timeline report

Finally, do not forget to apply time stamps from email activity (if it exists) as well.

A classroom exercise of timeline analysis is provided in Appendix C.

3

Case Study

From my experience as an instructor, I know that not everyone learns from just reading about concepts. Most people learn more when they are engaged with real-life situations and are allowed to get to their hands dirty.

This section will provide information from an actual case study. You will then use that information to prepare a report in the next section.

 Throughout this section, you will see checkpoints. These checkpoints are topics and questions for classroom discussion purposes.

Situation

You are tasked as a forensic examiner to conduct analysis of an HP netbook computer that had been seized during a search warrant. The suspect associated with the search warrant was involved in a peer-to-peer child pornography investigation.

Evidence

The HP netbook computer, serial number ABC12345, contained a Seagate 160 GB SATA hard drive, serial number 1ZY1234X.

A forensic image of the 160 GB hard drive was created using a Tableau T35es write-block device and EnCase version 6.19. The image was successfully created with zero errors.

Operating System

The installed operating system was Microsoft Windows 7, Starter Edition, with one active user account named "temp," which was originally created on 12/1/2009. A user profile named "temp" was created and files associated with that profile were stored in C:\Users\temp.

Figure 3-1 – Windows user profile

 CHECKPOINT

Is the user's account password-protected?

Did the user try to use hiding techniques, such as hidden folders?

Could the guest account or another account access notable files you find during your analysis?

The username of this account, which was originally called "temp," was later renamed to "Omar the Horrible." This account was password-protected.

The user's Pictures folder (My Pictures), contained a user-created hidden folder called ptxxx (Figure 3-2). This folder contained other subfolders, such as:

img

vid

2012 parade kids

my lil ones

Figure 3-2 – User's Pictures folder

The Guest account was enabled on 9/18/2010 and last used on 9/20/2010.

Windows 7 runs a service known as Volume Shadow Copy (VSC), which makes an incremental backup of the user's data. By restoring the data from each VSC, you may be able to find potentially relevant information that had been deleted.

The System Volume Information folder in this image contained 15 VSC files created 12/26/2011 through 2/1/2012 (Figure 3-3).

Figure 3-3 – System Volume Information folder contains Volume Shadow Copy data

Installed Programs

A peer-to-peer file sharing program known as MP3 Rocket (version 5.4.7) was installed.

CHECKPOINT

Does the program auto-start?

Did the user change the default settings?

Can you locate any evidence of the user's search terms?

MP3 Rocket was not configured to auto-start when the user logged in and required the user to manually start the program to run it.

The user has the ability to define specific folders that completed downloads can be stored based on media type. In this case, the user defined specific folders for images and videos (Figure 3-4):

C:\Users\temp\Pictures\ptxxx\img

C:\Users\temp\Pictures\ptxxx\vid

Figure 3-4 – Partial listing of data found within Downloads.dat file

This P2P program uses a file called downloads.dat (Figure 3-5) to keep track of the files the user has selected for download. In this version of MP3 Rocket, this file also stores the user's search terms. In this case, the file contained the following user search terms:

9yo

pthc black

pedo dad

The user also searched specifically for videos using MP3 Rocket using the following 8 search terms:

9yo

pthc black

8yo

toddler

3yo toddler girl

pedo dad

2yo

pthc family

```
118113 idth__t··640xt·)http://www.limewire.com/schemas/video.xsdsq·~·F?@·········w········
118193 ·q·~·Kt·;7441B2A3CD81B41E6C0CDCEADE9B3200;fwt/1;50858:173.48.134.134q·~·Yq·~·[xx
118273 xq·~·¯sq·~·F?@········w·········q·~·}sq·~·Î····y··q·~·Ôq·~·Kq·~·|q·~·|q·~·|sq·~·±
118353 t·}C:\Users\temp\Pictures\ptxxx\vid\········girl·-·REAL-········
118433 ······with sound (Pthc,Pedo,Child Baby······).aviw·\xq·~·|sq·~·F?@·····w········
118513 ···t··searchInformationMapsq·~·F?@·········w·········t··xmlt·|<?xml version="1.0"?><
118593 videos xsi:noNamespaceSchemaLocation="http://www.limewire.com/schemas/video.xsd"
118673 ><video title="pedo dad"/></videos>t··titlet··pedo dadt··typesq·~·ß····t··mediaq
118753 ·~·ät··queryt··pedo dadxxxxsq·~·sq·~·w······?@········sq·~··········r··*······
118833 ·A¦·····öq·~·Vt··134463.mpegq·~·Xsq·~·sq·~·sq·~·sq·~·w+)urn:sha1:3WVTHAJGHYX
118913 LVGK5675MBE22W3FQKYSFq·~·xq·~·]uq·~·B····sq·~·D····sq·~·F?@·········w········t··v
118993 ideos__video__length__t··477t··videos__video__height__t··288t··videos__video__wi
119073 dth__t··352xq·~·sq·~·F?@·········w·········q·~·Kt··98ED597F4E5DD3468DE0D1603BD8FF0
119153 0q·~·Yq·~·[xxxq·~·sq·~·F?@·········w·········q·~·Nsq·~·Î·····A¦·q·~·q·~·|q·~·Pt··
119233 134463.mpegq·~·Rsq·~·±t·#C:\Users\temp\Downloads\134463.mpegw·\xq·~·ªsq·~·F?@··
119313 ·········w·········xxxsq·~·sq·~·w······?@········sq·~···········Oi·······ø00··
```

Figure 3-5 – Search terms are found within Downloads.dat file (portions redacted)

CHECKPOINT

Did the user preview any files during the download process?

Searching for deleted downloads.dat records in unallocated space may yield the names of files that the user was intentionally trying to download. This type of data recovery helps to demonstrate the user's intent on types of files that were selected for download.

In addition to the normal P2P download activity, the user previewed movies during the download process. This was found during the review of the VSC dated 12/26/11 (Figure 3-6).

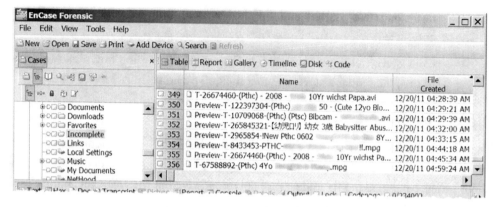

Figure 3-6 – Incomplete folder restored from VSC shows user was actively previewing downloads

Digital Videos

The "vid" folder (C:\Users\temp\pictures\ptxxx\vid) contained 158 digital movies of which 150 depict child pornography (Figure 3-7).

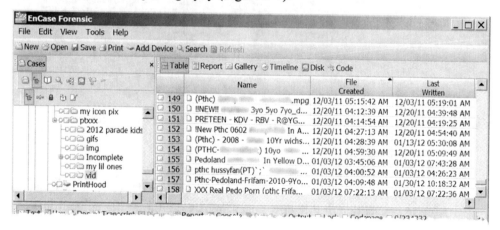

Figure 3-7 – Downloaded videos were stored in a separate user-created folder

CHECKPOINT

For P2P software like this version, the file creation time is the time the download was started and the last written time is when the download completed.

Consider providing a complete listing of all files in the download folder(s) to give the reader a sense of what the download activity looked like.

Digital Photographs

The "img" folder (C:\Users\temp\pictures\ptxxx\img) contained 824 digital photographs of which 800 depict child pornography and child erotica. Not all of the photographs contained in this folder were downloaded using MP3 Rocket (Figure 3-8).

Figure 3-8 – Downloaded images were stored in a separate user-created folder

CHECKPOINT

The filenames for some of the files in the IMG folder does not fit the usual file naming convention of P2P downloads. Where did these files come from?

All of these suspect child pornographic videos and photographs depicted naked prepubescent and/or partially clothed boys and/or girls engaged in sexual situations with other similarly aged boys and/or girls and/or with an adult male or female. Some of these videos and photographs also depicted naked prepubescent and/or partially clothed boys and/or girls provocatively posing alone or with other similarly aged boys or girls.

Personal Documents and Email

There were no personal documents associated with the defendant, such as journals, letters, resumes, tax documents, or work-related documents.

A folder in the user's profile (C:\Users\temp\Pictures\my icon pix) contained personal photographs of the defendant (Figure 3-9).

Figure 3-9 – Personal photographs were stored in a user-created folder

Client-based email was not found on the hard drive. Internet history indicated that the user was using Hotmail's web-based email service with an email address of [redacted]@hotmail.com. Email associated with this account was not located or recovered.

IMGSRC.RU Website

The user's Internet Explorer cached data contained filenames found in the "img" folder. The files stored in the cache folders are tracked with an index.dat file (Figure 3-10). The files came from a website with the URL of http://imgsrc.ru.

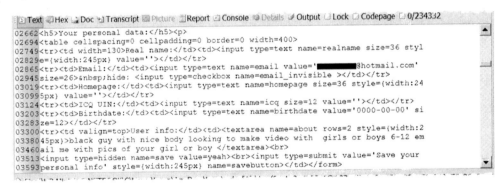

Figure 3-10 – Index.dat file contains information about a cached file

A cached HTML page (Figure 3-11) showed that a user account for the website was created on 1/4/2011 and was associated with the email address of [redacted]@hotmail.com. This user profile described the person as *"guy with nice body looking to make video with girls or boys 6-12 email me with pics of your girl or boy"*

Figure 3-11 – Cached HTML file

The user created two online photo albums at the site with the following descriptions:

1) "cropped nude pics of myself (eze) (password protected)"(created on 1/23/2012)

2) "sexy kids at a parade (no nude)" (created on 1/23/2012)

The first album matched images found on the hard drive in the user's profile in the following folder: C:\Users\temp\Pictures\my icon pix. This folder contained personal photographs of the defendant.

The second album matched images found on the hard drive in the user's profile in the following folder: C:\Users\temp\Pictures\ptxxx\2012 parade kids (Figure 3-12).This folder contains 25 digital photos, which were taken on 1/2/2012 at the Rose Parade. This set of 25 photos were extracted from a larger set of 171 photos taken at the parade using a SONY·DSC-T300 camera, which were in the following folder: C:\Users\temp\Pictures\2012 Rose Parade.

Figure 3-12 – Digital photographs taken with a Sony camera were copied to a user-created folder

 CHECKPOINT

Locating search terms helps to demonstrate the user's intent.

A cached HTML page (Figure 3-13) shows that the website had been searched for the following search terms and criteria:

kids (in section) nudity

boys (in section) nudity

girls (in section) nudity

naked (in section) kids

natural (in section) kids

bath (in section) kids

```
[:] Text  Hex  Doc  Transcript  Picture  Report  Console  Details  Output  Lock  Codepage  0/234332
04552<option value='32'>&middot; rollerblades</option>
04602<option value='28'>&middot; strikeball</option>
04650<option value='12'>&middot; football</option>
04696<option value='13'>&middot; hockey</option>
04740<option value='69'>transportation</option>
04783<option value='35'>hobby</option>
04817<option value='33'>&middot; collection</option>
04865<option value='39'>&middot; fishing</option>
04910<option value='27'>funpics</option>
04946</select></form><h1>Search results for 'girls' in section 'nudity':</h1><p>
05022<table width=99% cellpadding=1 cellspacing=1>
05068<tr><th width=620 align=left>name (<a href=/main/switch.php?show=pix&cnt=%2Fmain
05148%2Fsearch.php%3Fstr%3Dgirls%26cat%3D24>show album previews</a>)</th><th width=30
05228>photos</th><th width=110 align=right>in section</th><th width=150 align=right>m
05308odified</th></tr>
05326<tr valign=top class=tdd><td><a target=_blank href=/grcc/a715847.html>grcc: OLD
```

Figure 3-13 – Cached HTML page containing user's search terms

The user's Internet activity was limited since Internet Explorer had been configured to "Delete browsing history on exit" (Figure 3-14).

Figure 3-14 – User settings for Internet Explorer

Malware Detection

Microsoft Security Essentials was installed and functioning (Figure 3-15). There were no "harmful" items detected or listed. The software was up-to-date as of 2/1/2012 (virus and spyware definition version 1.119.1184.0 installed).

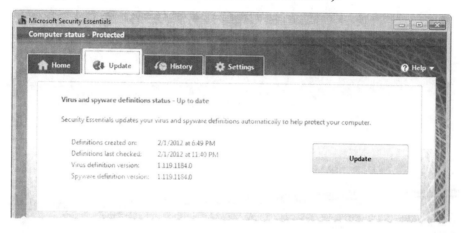

Figure 3-15 – Definition information for Microsoft Security Essentials

A virus scan of the hard drive was conducted using ESET NOD32 Antivirus (version 3.0.695.0, virus signature database 6872). The results of this scan identified no viruses or malware.

4

Writing Your Report

From a workflow perspective of writing your expert report, conduct your analysis first. Your analysis will help you to prepare an outline of your report. Once your analysis is completed, think about your findings from an objective viewpoint and then begin to insert that information into your outline.

I will start by showing you the main subject headings of a sample expert report. This sample is not intended to imply that if you do not follow it, then you are violating some official formatting style. This sample is a guideline for you to follow. If you remember your target audience, you will see that these headings will help guide the reader through your report. Disjointed information randomly placed throughout your report does not help reader comprehension.

The main subject headings of our sample expert report are:

A. Summary

B. Introduction

C. List of Data Reviewed and Methodology

D. Summary of Opinions

E. Detailed Analysis to Support Opinions

F. Exhibits

So, where do you start? We have often been told "at the beginning." However, in this situation, I want you to skip past the first three sections and start reviewing your

analysis to write the outline of Section D (Summary of Opinions). The first three sections seem easy to start drafting and you may be asking, "why skip past them?" The simple answer is that once you have completed Sections D through F, you will have all of the information needed to complete the first three sections.

You may also find that as you prepare your detailed analysis narrative, you may find a need to conduct some follow-up analysis.

As you begin to write, use short and concise paragraphs. Some of the information you will be reporting can be very technical. Having long, detailed, run-on paragraphs will only help to confuse the reader.

Summary of Opinions

By reviewing your analysis, what are your expert opinions? I will emphasize again that these opinions are not based on wild guesses; they need to be based on your analysis and your objective findings. Since you are objective, you did not start your analysis with opinions that were predetermined.

At this time, review the case study in Section 3 and draft the language for at least two opinions:

Opinion 1

Opinion 2

Here are two sample opinions that may be used for this section:

Summary of Opinions

Opinion 1

The defendant's computer was running peer-to-peer software, which was used to intentionally download digital photographs and movies that depicted child pornography from other computers on the Internet. While the movies were being downloaded, the user previewed portions of those movies and then allowed to the movies to complete the download process.

Opinion 2

The defendant's computer was used to create a user account for a Russian website that is maintained for the purpose of hosting and sharing digital photographs. Personal photographs of the defendant along with photographs of children taken during the 2012 Rose Parade were uploaded to the website and associated those images with this user account. The website was searched with words associated with children and nudity. Digital photographs depicting child pornography and child erotica were intentionally downloaded from this website and stored in a specific user-created folder that would allow the peer-to-peer software to share those images with other people on the Internet.

Detailed Analysis

Now that your opinions have been defined based on your objective findings, it is time to report all of the facts from your analysis that support these opinions in this section.

It would be simple to take the case study information that was provided in Section 3 and copy it into this section. While that would not be a completed representation of your detailed analysis, it would be a good outline to help you get started. An outline is always a good way to start.

A real challenge for the writer is how to explain the analysis and findings in a simple way for the reader to understand. Additionally, the writer needs to think ahead in how it could be explained to the jury.

From my trial and teaching experience, I found that that the best way to explain some things is to associate your findings with things the average person would

understand. Most people have a computer, so the more that you can demonstrate visually with that of a normal computer user's experience, the easier it will be for them to understand your message.

As the old adage states, "a picture is worth a thousand words," and it is a great way to convey your message. While you are writing your report, think about what screenshots you could create and add as exhibits that would make your story simple. At the appropriate times in your report, direct the reader's attention to those exhibits.

Another benefit of adding those screenshots to your report is that they can be used during trial as demonstrative exhibits. Since they are already in your report, the opposing side will already have them and there will not be an issue of failing to comply with discovery. In one trial, the defense objected to the demonstrative exhibit being offered by the prosecution; however, once it was pointed out that the same graphic appeared in my report (which the defense had already received months earlier), the exhibit was allowed.

It is now time to introduce the reader to the environment you analyzed. A good starting point is the operating system. What did the user see when he started his computer? Did he have to use a password to login? What did the desktop environment look like? These are very simple to demonstrate when you use VMware.

Here is a simple example: You know the defendant's computer required a password during the login process. How do you know a password was required? You could use forensic software that has a script which would tell you the user account was password-protected, but how do you know for sure? You could look at the SAM registry hive for the specific user subkey and then the specific value data. After all, it is good to know where this information comes from. But how are you going to explain this?

A simple screenshot of the login window displayed within VMware will show it instantly.

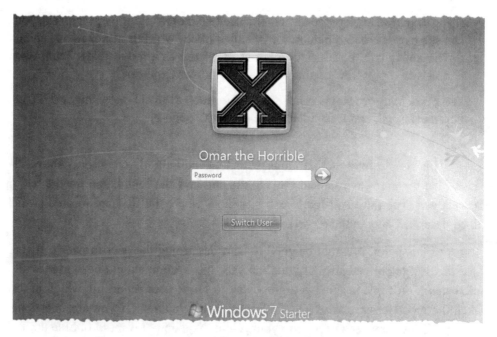

It is now time to jump in and tell the reader a story about your findings. Start by laying a foundation that you will build upon.

Detailed Analysis

The defendant's computer had Windows 7 Starter Edition installed as the operating system. When first prompted to create a new user account, the username of "temp" was used on 12/1/2009. That username was later modified to "Omar the Horrible." However, since the username was first called "temp," a user profile named "temp" was created and files associated with that profile were stored in C:\Users\temp.

The Guest account was enabled on 9/18/2010 and last used on 9/20/2010. The Guest account does not have access to the temp account or files within the temp profile.

The temp account (aka "Omar the Horrible") was password-protected. The Windows login screen is attached as Exhibit A.

Once logged in as "Omar the Horrible," the user's desktop appeared, which is attached as Exhibit B.

Using Windows Explorer to display the user's Pictures folder (My Pictures), you can see a user-created hidden folder called ptxxx, which is attached as Exhibit C. The ability to see this hidden folder (depicted as a faded folder icon) was enabled by the user through a setting in Windows Explorer.

The ptxxx folder contains other subfolders, such as my lil ones, img, vid, 2012 parade kids, gif, and Incomplete (see Exhibit C, page 2).

This simple introduction along with four exhibits of screenshots shows the reader what the user environment looked like and lays the foundation for the rest of your analysis. The third and fourth exhibits show where the files are located (which will be described later in the report).

At this point, it would be good to start describing the peer-to-peer software. Since this is a major category of your analysis, this section should be started with a topic heading. A topic heading is a great way to break your report up, which in turn makes the report easy to read and find specific information. If you are questioned during trial, you may need to refer to your report. You do not want to fumble through pages of your report trying to find specific information.

MP3 Rocket

MP3 Rocket is a peer-to-peer file sharing program. Version 5.4.7 was the current version installed on the defendant's hard drive.

MP3 Rocket was not configured to auto-start when the user logged in and required the user to manually start the program to run it.

This version of MP3 Rocket has the same functionality of an open-source peer-to-peer program known as Limewire. In testing this version of the software in a controlled environment, I found it to function the same way as Limewire in the way that you could search, download, preview downloads in progress, view completed downloads, and configure the program.

When MP3 Rocket is first installed, it creates one folder for downloading files (Incomplete) and one folder for sharing files (Shared). When a user selects a file to download, a temporary file is created in the Incomplete folder. The

temporary file is given a prefix to the original file name. The prefix consists of the letter T and a number, which is the file size (total number of bytes or characters within the file). An example would be "T-20265280-The Lord of the Rings – The Hobbit 2006 Trailer.mpeg."

Once the file has completed downloading, the filename prefix is removed and it is moved from the Incomplete folder and stored in the Shared folder.

The user has the ability to define specific folders that completed downloads can be stored based on media type. In this case, the user defined specific folders for images and videos:

C:\Users\temp\Pictures\ptxxx\img

C:\Users\temp\Pictures\ptxxx\vid

A screenshot showing the user settings is displayed in Exhibit D, page 1.

When the user makes this change, the user is then prompted to share these new folders. The prompt the user would see is displayed in Exhibit D, page 2.

The user has the option to share or not share these folders. On the defendant's computer, the user clicked OK to add these folders to be shared. A screenshot showing the settings for Shared Folders is displayed in Exhibit D, page 3.

To provide a simple depiction of the running software, I created screenshots of MP3 Rocket. These screenshots are attached as Exhibit E.

Exhibit E, Page 1, shows the Search Tab for All Types of files. From this tab, the user could select a specific file type that he was interested in finding (such as an image or video) and then type a search term(s). This also shows the incomplete files that had been selected for download, but have not finished downloading.

During the download, the user has the option to preview the file before the file has completed downloading. For example, if a video file was 22% complete, the user would click on the Preview button. The software creates a copy of the in-progress download and adds the prefix of "Preview-" to the filename. This allows the user to watch the partially downloaded video file, while the remainder of the video continues to download.

Exhibit E, Page 2, shows the My Files Tab and a partial listing of the files stored in the shared folder named "img."

> Exhibit E, Page 3, shows the My Files Tab and a partial listing of the files stored in the shared folder named "vid."

Now that you have explained the basics of the peer-to-peer software interface, you will want to explain your findings regarding the downloaded images and videos. This subsection could start with a new topic heading, such as Download Activity.

Download Activity

Typically, files that exist in the user's P2P shared folder(s) originated from one of two activities:

1) The user downloaded the file using peer-to-peer software from others across the Internet.

2) The user copied the file from his personal collection of data.

Understanding the process of how files are retrieved from other users across the Internet using MP3 Rocket and what artifacts are created from that activity will help to establish evidence of downloading.

Files that are being downloaded with MP3 Rocket are given a temporary filename, which consists of a prefix (T-#######-) and the original filename. These files are stored in the Incomplete directory.

Individual entries for each incomplete file, including the hash value, are listed within a file named "downloads.dat," which is a file maintained by MP3 Rocket. The downloads.dat file is constantly being updated while MP3 Rocket is running and downloading files.

The file creation time of the file being downloaded is the time that the file was selected by the user to be downloaded. As blocks of blocks of data are downloaded and added to that file, the last written time of the file is updated.

Once the download is complete, the file is renamed by MP3 Rocket to its original filename and moved to the designated Shared directory. The last written time of the file is when the file finished downloading.

The Downloads.dat file in this version of MP3 Rocket also stores the user's search terms. In this case, the downloads.dat file contained the following user search terms:

9yo

pthc black

pedo dad

The user also searched specifically for videos using MP3 Rocket using the following 8 search terms:

9yo

pthc black

8yo

toddler

3yo toddler girl

pedo dad

2yo

pthc family

A file listing of the Incomplete folder (C:\Users\temp\Incomplete) is attached as Exhibit F. The file created time of the file is when the user selected the file to be downloaded using MP3 Rocket. The last written time is the last time a block of data associated with the file had been downloaded.

A file listing of the vid folder (C:\Users\temp\pictures\ptxxx\vid) is attached as Exhibit G. This folder contained 158 digital movies of which 150 depict child pornography.

A file listing of the img folder (C:\Users\temp\pictures\ptxxx\img) is attached as Exhibit H. This folder contained 824 digital photographs of which 800 depict child pornography and child erotica. It should be noted that not all of the photographs contained in this folder were downloaded using MP3 Rocket.

Volume Shadow Copy

Windows 7 runs a service known as Volume Shadow Copy, which makes a differential backup of the data on a volume, which includes user-created files. Shadow copies of data can provide a time capsule view of a volume at a particular time, which can be used to demonstrate how files have been altered or deleted. In reviewing this service, I found that the service created backups at the following dates and times:

12/26/11 02:02:17 PM (MP3 Rocket activity)

12/30/11 02:48:03 AM

01/02/12 01:52:05 PM

01/02/12 03:23:13 PM

01/02/12 03:50:40 PM

01/06/12 12:15:38 PM (MP3 Rocket activity)

01/06/12 04:00:16 PM

01/10/12 11:19:59 AM

01/11/12 04:53:20 PM

01/16/12 03:09:35 PM (MP3 Rocket activity)

01/19/12 06:50:53 PM

01/22/12 07:40:35 PM

01/25/12 03:36:56 PM (MP3 Rocket activity)

01/29/12 05:42:39 PM

02/01/12 11:39:38 PM (MP3 Rocket activity)

I reviewed each backup that may have captured any activity associated with MP3 Rocket and noted it in the above list. After that review, I restored the data from those dates and conducted further analysis.

From the restored volume shadow copy backup dated 12/26/2011, I could see the user's P2P download activity in the Incomplete folder. Based on the activity in that folder, I could see the user actively downloading files and previewing downloads-in-progress (see Exhibit I).

From the restored volume shadow copy backup dated 1/6/2012, I could see new user P2P activity in the Incomplete folder. Exhibit J displays the folder activity.

In Exhibits I and J, I found examples of previewed downloads-in-progress where the downloads were allowed to continue until completion (these items were highlighted in the exhibits). The completed files were located in the current vid folder (C:\Users\temp\pictures\ptxxx\vid). By using the information from the restored volume shadow copy backup data (specifically Exhibits I and J), I was

able to create a timeline that demonstrates the following activity for 16 digital movies that depict child pornography:

1. When the user selected the file for download

2. When the user previewed the file while the download was in progress

3. When the download completed

This timeline is represented in Exhibit K.

At this point, you should review what you have written to ensure that your documentation supports Opinion 1.

If you are satisfied, then move on to writing about your detailed analysis to support Opinion 2 and start with a new topic heading.

IMGSRC.RU Website

As stated earlier, not all of the photographs contained in the img folder (C:\Users\temp\pictures\ptxxx\img) were downloaded using MP3 Rocket. Based on the file naming convention, and the date/time stamps, it appeared that the files had been copied directly from a website.

By conducting a search of the user's Internet Explorer cached data for filenames found in the img folder, I found evidence that the files came from a website with the URL of http://imgsrc.ru. I am familiar with this specific website. This website offers a free service as a digital photo hosting service, which is located in Russia. The site allows people to search the "photo albums" of other users and post digital photos of their own. In order to post pictures, a user must register with a valid email address. After completing the basic registration information, the site sends an email containing the login password to the user.

By searching the user's cached Internet Explorer data, I found that the user created an account using the email address of *[redacted]*@hotmail.com. I found cached webpages that matched the live website page for the user's profile. A copy of the live webpage is attached as Exhibit L.

Both the live webpage and the cached page shows the user account of *[redacted]* was created on 2/4/2011 and the user info states *"guy with nice body*

looking to make video with girls or boys 6-12 email me with pics of your girl or boy"

The user created two online photo albums at the site with the following descriptions:

1. "cropped nude pics of myself (eze) (password protected)," which was created on 1/23/2012.

2. "sexy kids at a parade (no nude)," which was created on 1/23/2012.

The first album matched images found on the hard drive in the user's profile in the following folder: C:\Users\temp\Pictures\my icon pix. This folder contains additional photos of the defendant.

The second album matched images found on the hard drive in the user's profile in the following folder: C:\Users\temp\Pictures\ptxxx\2012 parade kids. This folder contains 25 digital photos, which were taken on 1/2/2012 at the Rose Parade and copied to the computer on 1/2/2012. This set of 25 photos were extracted from a larger set of 171 photos taken at the parade using a SONY·DSC-T300 camera, which were in the following folder: C:\Users\temp\Pictures\2012 Rose Parade.

To search the website, a person can enter search terms and limit the results to a specific section, such as travel, family, and hobby. By searching the user's cache and HTML code found in unallocated space of the hard drive, I found that the user had been searching the website for photo albums using the following search terms and criteria:

kids (in section) nudity

boys (in section) nudity

girls (in section) nudity

naked (in section) kids

natural (in section) kids

bath (in section) kids

An example of a HTML search page found in the user's cache folder (C:\Users\temp\AppData\Local\Microsoft\Windows\Temporary Internet Files\Low\Content.IE5\7DYJ9765\search[1].htm) is attached as Exhibit M.

The cached web pages found on the hard drive indicated that the user was logged into the website (see Exhibit M as an example). In order to log in, you have to use a password which is sent to your registered email address.

The user then previewed photo albums based on the search criteria and saved specific photos to the img folder using the right-click, *Save picture as...* function of Internet Explorer.

It should be noted that not all of the user's Internet activity could be reported since Internet Explorer had been configured to *Delete browsing history on exit.*

In closing, your report may include information about any type of malware that was detected during your analysis.

Malware Detection

Microsoft Security Essentials was installed and functioning on the defendant's computer. There were no "harmful" items detected or listed. The software was up-to-date as of 2/1/2012 (virus and spyware definition version 1.119.1184.0 installed).

I conducted a separate virus scan of the hard drive using ESET NOD32 Antivirus (version 3.0.695.0, virus signature database 6872). The results of this scan identified no viruses or malware.

Exhibits

Once the narrative has been completed, it is a good idea to build a single table that lists all of the exhibits that were created. This provides a quick reference to both you and the reader. This is the last section of your report.

Exhibits

This report contains the following exhibits:

Exhibit A	Windows login screen
Exhibit B	User's desktop
Exhibit C	Windows Explorer, Pictures folder
Exhibit D	MP3 Rocket – Options
Exhibit E	MP3 Rocket – User Interface
Exhibit F	Incomplete folder file listing
Exhibit G	vid folder file listing
Exhibit H	img folder file listing
Exhibit I	Incomplete folder file listing from backup dated 12/26/2011
Exhibit J	Incomplete folder file listing from backup dated 1/6/2012
Exhibit K	Timeline of download and preview activity for specific videos
Exhibit L	Screenshot of live website imgsrc.ru matching cached page found on hard drive
Exhibit M	Cached user profile web page
Exhibit N	Cached search web page

For reference purposes, portions of these exhibits are located at the end of Report #1 in Appendix A of this handbook. Some of the multi-page exhibits have been redacted and reduced to a single page.

Summary

Now that the narrative of your detailed analysis is complete, it is time to write a summary, which is the first section of your report. The summary should be brief and to the point. The summary is a great way to prepare the reader and help them understand what the rest of your report is about.

The following is a sample summary that could be used for this report.

Summary

I have conducted a computer forensic examination of the hard drive contained within the defendant's computer, which was seized pursuant to a search warrant. Based on my analysis, I found that the computer had been used to intentionally download digital photographs and videos depicting child pornography using peer-to-peer software. Additionally, I found that the computer had been used to intentionally download digital photographs depicting child pornography from a Russian photo sharing website.

Introduction

The second section of your report is the introduction. In this section, provide a simple explanation to the reader about how you became involved in the matter and what you were requested to do. This section should also include the authority for your exam, such as a search warrant.

Introduction

On June 15, 2012, I was requested to conduct a computer forensic examination of a Hewlett Packard (HP) netbook computer that was seized pursuant to a search warrant dated June 12, 2012. The defendant associated with the search warrant was involved in an undercover peer-to-peer child pornography investigation conducted by a federal law enforcement agency. The scope of my analysis was to review the defendant's hard drive and provide a written report of my findings.

List of Data Reviewed and Methodology

You're almost done. Your analysis is complete and now you need to tell the reader what you reviewed during your analysis and the methodology you used. This should also include the software you used during your analysis.

List of Data Reviewed and Methodology

My analysis and report is based, in part, on my education, training, and experience in the field of computer forensics and law enforcement.

I have read the initial report documenting the undercover investigation and the search warrant dated June 12, 2012.

On June 15, 2012, I received the defendant's HP netbook computer (model Mini 110, serial number ABC12345). This computer contained a Seagate 160 GB SATA hard drive, serial number 1ZY1234X.

I created a forensic image of the 160 GB hard drive using a Tableau T35es write-block device and EnCase version 6.19. The image was successfully created with zero errors.

I examined the forensic image using EnCase Forensic Edition (version 6.19.4), which is a commercially available program.

At the start and conclusion of my analysis, I verified the MD5 hash value for the forensic image (ABC80097BC008570D5F9CA65BDB10B40) and zero errors were detected.

During my analysis, I used VMware (version 8.04), which is a commercially available program, to run the forensic image of the hard drive in a virtual environment. This environment allowed me to use the operating system and installed software in the same manner as it would appear on the HP computer. Using this environment, I was able to create screenshots to demonstrate activity as it would have appeared on the actual computer.

During my analysis, I extracted data from the Windows Volume Shadow Copy files by mounting the forensic image as a physical disk and using the dd imaging utility from the Forensic Acquisition Utilities (build 1.3.0.2390) distributed by GMG Systems, Inc. This utility is a publically available program.

In the Detailed Analysis and Methodology sections, I referred to a service called Volume Shadow Copy (VSC), which is available on Windows Vista and Windows 7. Since VSC acts similar to a time capsule, it allows you to go back in time and look at a user's activity. Needless to say, this service may contain extremely valuable evidence in a case and should not be overlooked. In this case, the VSC data contained information that helped prepare a timeline of the user's download activity.

While I described the method used to extract VSC data in this particular case, you should be aware that there are different techniques to obtain this data. This specific method used a publicly available tool to extract the data from each VSC entry and requires a lot of disk space. Basically you need to make a separate dd image for each VSC entry. In this case, the hard drive had a capacity of 160GB hard drive and 15 VSC entries. If you wanted to extract each entry, you would need about 2.4 TB of disk space to store the 15 dd images. A commercially available tool that has recently become available and does not require a complete extraction of each VSC entry is called Reconoittre by Sanderson Forensics. Reconnoittre is a tool that I have personally tested and added to my forensic toolbox.

Now that you have completed all of the sections of your report, organize your report in the same order as the major sections listed at the beginning of this section:

A. Summary

B. Introduction

C. List of Data Reviewed and Methodology

D. Summary of Opinions

E. Detailed Analysis to Support Opinions

F. Exhibits

5

Inside the Courtroom

Since I started conducting computer forensic examinations, I have had some opportunities to testify in both State and Federal court as an expert witness. I soon realized that testifying in these cases was much different than testifying in criminal cases when I was a patrol officer or a detective. As a patrol officer, I testified about topics such as what I saw when I arrived at a scene or where I found a piece of evidence. There may have been a little cross-examination, but it was pretty straightforward and I was not on the stand for hours.

I have met many forensic examiners over the years while I was either teaching or attending a conference that never had to testify about their work in court. As most examiners would agree, testifying in court as an expert witness is probably the biggest challenge in their field. Examiners understand where to look during their analysis, but having to explain that to other people can be difficult. Furthermore, since many examiners have never been called to testify as an expert witness, they do not know what to expect or what types of questions they could be asked by counsel.

When you think about all of the training you have attended, how much training have you received in regards to testifying? The majority of you may respond with "very little."

In this section, I wanted to pass along helpful tips for an examiner that will be testifying in court. However, before I get started, I want to be clear that I am neither an attorney nor do I teach law. I definitely would not consider myself a professional

witness. I am simply providing some insight based on my experiences and from others I have met over the years.

Jury Instructions

Before the jury deliberates, the judge will provide the jury with a set of instructions. Each jurisdiction has different jury instructions and there are instructions for civil cases and criminal cases. As you prepare to testify, I want you to consider the instructions the jury will be given about witness testimony. The jury will be considering these instructions as they review their notes and deliberate.

As an example, the Ninth Circuit Model Criminal Jury Instructions provides two instructions for witnesses: Section 3.9 (Credibility of Witnesses) and Section 4.14 (Opinion Evidence, Expert Witness).

3.9 Credibility of Witnesses

In deciding the facts in this case, you may have to decide which testimony to believe and which testimony not to believe. You may believe everything a witness says, or part of it, or none of it.

In considering the testimony of any witness, you may take into account:

(1) the witness's opportunity and ability to see or hear or know the things testified to;

(2) the witness's memory;

(3) the witness's manner while testifying;

(4) the witness's interest in the outcome of the case, if any;

(5) the witness's bias or prejudice, if any;

(6) whether other evidence contradicted the witness's testimony;

(7) the reasonableness of the witness's testimony in light of all the evidence; and

(8) any other factors that bear on believability.

The weight of the evidence as to a fact does not necessarily depend on the number of witnesses who testify. What is important is how believable the witnesses were, and how much weight you think their testimony deserves.

4.14 Opinion Evidence, Expert Witness

You have heard testimony from persons who, because of education or experience, were permitted to state opinions and the reasons for their opinions.

Such opinion testimony should be judged like any other testimony. You may accept it or reject it, and give it as much weight as you think it deserves, considering the witness's education and experience, the reasons given for the opinion, and all the other evidence in the case.

You also need to be aware that not only will the jury consider these instructions, you will likely see opposing counsel use some of these instructions as tactics against you.

Now that you have reviewed these instructions, think about how the jury will view you during your testimony. What was your demeanor while testifying? Were you confident or defensive?

Do you have an interest in the outcome of the case? Were you biased or prejudiced in any way? While you may not be biased or have an interest in the outcome, opposing counsel may try to paint that picture to the jury.

In my experience, I have had opposing counsel raise the question about how much I was being paid for my testimony. Counsel was trying to paint the picture that my opinion was for sale or I had some type of interest in the outcome of the case. I am used to this and have learned to expect it. As soon as the line of questioning about being paid to testify starts, I think to myself, "oh, here it comes."

Q: Are you being paid to testify today?

A: I am not being paid for my testimony. I am being paid for my time.

Q: Approximately how many hours have you worked on this investigation?

A: About 30 hours.

Q: Is your compensation affected by whether or not you testify as an expert at trial?

A: No.

Q: Is your compensation in any way affected by the outcome of this trial?

A: Not at all.

Effective Testimony

You will want to be effective in how you present information to the jury. As I mentioned earlier, your role is to take complex findings and explain them in clear and understandable terms. You already started this by effectively writing your report in that manner.

When you are asked a question, turn to the jury and explain your answer. Make eye contact with them. Based on their body language, does it appear that they understand what you are saying? Think about your body language as well. Are you relaxed and confident? A friend of mine sat through all of my testimony one day and I asked him what he thought after we walked out of the courtroom. He described my demeanor as "someone who was sitting down with family at Thanksgiving and telling everyone a story that they all wanted to hear." Personally, that was great feedback for me. I now pass that description on to anyone who asks me about how to engage the jury.

I found that using analogies and demonstrative exhibits are the best way to describe your findings. What are some everyday encounters that the jury may be able to identify or associate to your findings? If you were trying to describe how you recovered files from a hard drive, do you tell the jury that you found a file signature of a JPEG photo at a specific physical sector on the hard drive and then copied 210,092 bytes to the end of the file?

Explaining your findings in simple terms may be very challenging though. Here is an example of an analogy that could be used to describe the file recovery process on a hard drive:

When you go into a library, there are thousands of books on the shelves. Think of files on a hard drive as books in a library. When you want to find a book, you go to the card catalog to find the name of the book, the author, and determine what row and shelf contains the book. The same is true for a hard drive except the card catalog is called the master file table. The master file table will tell you the name of the file, dates and times, and what folder contains the file. If someone deletes the file, the file does not disappear right away; it still exists. If this was a library, what really happened is the entry in the card catalog disappeared, but the book is still on the shelf. If you walk down to the same row and shelf, you can pull the book off the shelf and it is still intact. When I recovered the file using my forensic software, it is equivalent to walking down to that shelf, picking up the book, and reading it.

With any analogy that you plan to use, practice them with people who do not understand what you do and see if they understand your explanation.

If you are well-prepared and know your subject matter, you will be able to confidently tell the jury about your findings. Just remember that you are there to teach the jury, but not lecture them. Lectures are boring and may be condescending. The jury may have been through listening to other witnesses in the case and may be bored by the time you take the stand. Do not let that worry you, because what you have to tell them is interesting (seriously, they are looking for something to get their attention).

I also want you to consider what the jury may be thinking about you as you testify. Do you appear nervous or biased? Do you appear to be telling the truth? Do they understand what you are saying or are you geeking out with a bunch of techno-babble?

Opposing Expert

Depending on the strategy of the opposing counsel in a case, they may or may not engage the services of an expert. Even if counsel engages an expert, this person may never testify in court and only be used in a consulting capacity. This is especially true of the defendant in a case since the burden of proof is on the plaintiff. If this happens, the consulting expert will be asked to review the evidence and your report. The expert will then prepare notes and questions for opposing counsel to be used in your cross-examination. Since the consulting expert will not be testifying, their report will likely not be written and submitted through the discovery process.

You also need to consider that since the consulting expert will review the evidence and your report to confirm your findings, their review may lead to the case being settled prior to trial. This is all the more reason for you to be effective in writing your forensic report.

In addition to reviewing your report, opposing counsel may pose situations or "theories" to their expert. The expert will then review the evidence to determine if the evidence is in line with those theories.

Unless the expert finds evidence that is completely contrary to your findings or exculpatory evidence, it is very likely that the opposing expert will not be called to the stand. However, the real twist comes when opposing counsel uses you to introduce evidence and testimony to support their case. In essence, you will become their expert witness during trial.

Cross-Examination

After your direct testimony, opposing counsel may use a strategy during cross-examination that I have seen many times. At the start of the cross-examination, opposing counsel will try to get you to corroborate or agree with their opinions of the case. At this stage, their questions will not be aggressive; after all, they want you to agree with them.

Here is an example of questions you may be faced with at the beginning of cross-examination:

Q: Sir, you prepared a report of your analysis in this case?

A: I did.

Q: In that report, you generated your conclusions and findings; correct?

A: I did.

Q: And you documented the scope of your analysis; correct?

A: Yes.

Q: When you prepared that report, you were trying to be accurate; right?

A: Yes.

Q: As an agent of the Government, you were asked to conduct a complete forensic analysis of computers that were the subject of a criminal case; correct?

A: Yes.

Based on this opening line of questioning, opposing counsel is setting the stage to show the jury that you were not accurate and that your report was not complete.

Listen to the Question

It is important that you listen to the questions that are being asked. Opposing counsel will be reading from a script of questions and possible answers that you may provide. The questions that are being posed may require you to ask for clarification. If so, ask for clarification and do not reply with a simple "yes" answer. If counsel really does not understand what he is asking you and is simply following a script, he will have a very difficult time clarifying the question.

During questioning, you may find that opposing counsel will try to limit your answers to a simple yes or no answer. Simple yes or no answers can be misleading and you do not want the jury to be misled. If opposing counsel is trying to limit your answers, let him know that you will not mislead the jury.

Q: Mr. McLain testified that regarding whether or not he used documents that were copied on the external drive. Are you saying that that was incorrect?

A: So --

Q: Yes or no, please?

A: I can't give you a "yes or no" answer.

Q: Well, you gave Mr. Smith "yes or no" answers when you were answering his questions about the external drive that Mr. McLain testified about, weren't you?

A: Well, what I said is, I can't give you a "yes or no" answer that could possibly mislead the jury. So I need to explain my answer.

Q: I'm going to ask you -- okay, please do.

At that point, opposing counsel thought for a second and then allowed the expert to give his answer.

Active Listening

There are times during cross-examination when counsel may ask a question that is not technically accurate. For example:

Q: Does an email have meta --, is it called metadata?

A: Yes.

Q: When an email is downloaded from the server using Microsoft Live Mail, a file is created which has a file name and the time stamps of that file are embedded within the email message, is that correct?

Counsel is looking for a simple "yes" answer, but that would not be a true statement. In this instance, counsel may have intended to say that the specific EML file has date and time stamps, such as the time stamps in the Master File Table, but these time stamps are not embedded within the email message. You could easily answer yes because counsel is having a difficult time with phrasing the question and you think you understand the intent of counsel's question. However, take a moment to think about what the court record will reflect. You will be answering yes to an incorrect statement and the record does not describe counsel's intent. How will that incorrect statement be used in the future?

It is important to actively listen to each word in counsel's question. Based on your answer, counsel may be setting the stage for follow-up questions based on your incorrect answer.

The correct response is to explain that the question is not correct and the answer is no. Counsel may either rephrase the question or just move on to the next question.

Ping Pong Match

During cross-examination, counsel may try to control the pace by setting a rhythm of quick questions and you replying with quick answers. To the jury (and the court reporter), this will appear as a ping pong match. While counsel may be trying to make quick points while keeping the jury's attention, you may inadvertently provide incorrect answers as you are trying to keep up with counsel's questions.

As the expert witness, you are in control of your answers. Take the time to actively listen to each word of counsel's question and then pause to reflect on providing a correct answer. Just like answering questions during your direct testimony, you should take the time to turn towards the jury when giving your answer.

If you are asked a question that requires an explanation, provide the explanation first and then the answer. While providing your explanation to the jury, be aware that counsel may interrupt you in an effort to control your answers. If that occurs, politely ask counsel if you can finish your answer.

Not In Your Report

During cross-examination, counsel may ask you a line of questioning to set the stage for information that may not be in your report. As the saying goes, "It's not about what is in your report. It's about what *is not* in your report." Here are some sample questions:

1) Have you have prepared a thorough and complete report?

2) If you found exculpatory information, would you include it in your report?

3) Did you include all objective findings in your report?

4) Have you included all of your observations in your report?

As I mentioned earlier in this handbook, a hard drive contains an overwhelming volume of data for you to be able to report on every bit. Furthermore, your analysis may be limited to the scope of a search warrant (if you do not get a chance to mention this fact, this is a good question to be brought up during re-direct).

After these types of questions, counsel may try to introduce exhibits in an effort to demonstrate you omitted exculpatory evidence. Here are two examples of questions counsel may ask during cross-examination and the responses to those questions:

1) Counsel asked why you failed to include the last accessed time of files listed in your exhibit. Counsel may be trying to show that someone never accessed specific files and you failed to mention this important fact. In your response, you turn toward the jury and explain that during your earlier testimony (as well as it is mentioned in your report) you stated that Windows 7 was the installed on the hard drive. Windows 7 has disabled the last accessed time stamp and you omitted it since it does not serve any evidentiary purpose.

2) Counsel asked why you failed to list the recently accessed files from Microsoft Media Player, but you did recover deleted history from Internet Explorer. Counsel may be trying to show that someone never played specific digital movies and you omitted it from your report. You explain to the jury that Media Player was not configured to store the recently played movies and you cannot recover information that was never stored in the first place.

Area of Expertise

When you are testifying, you need to stay within your area of expertise. During cross-examination, counsel may try to get you to speak on topics that are outside your area of formal training, experience, and expertise.

In one case, a new computer forensic examiner conducted a preliminary analysis that included imaging the hard drive and searching for basic information such as email and download activity. During his review, he conducted a simple scan for possible viruses and possible malware. The scan resulted in a file that was identified as a "heuristic Trojan virus." However, since he had very limited knowledge about Trojan viruses, he documented the finding in his report without providing an opinion. During his cross-examination, counsel asked him questions about the topic of Trojan viruses.

You may feel like you should have an answer to any question that is asked during cross-examination. However, you do not want to speculate during your testimony and you should not feel compelled to provide an answer. In this case, the examiner provided a correct response by telling counsel that the subject was outside his area of expertise and he could not offer any opinions on the subject.

Typographical Errors

Opposing counsel may point out typographical errors in your report. This is a simple attempt to show you are sloppy in your work and you make mistakes. People make mistakes and you need to admit to them.

> **Q:** You made a mistake, didn't you?
>
> **A:** Yes. That page contained a typographical error and I did not catch it when I proofread my report. It should have read January 2011 and not January 2001. I will be writing a supplemental report to correct that error.

Losing Your Temper

One strategy that opposing counsel may try to use against you is to agitate or upset you. This can be achieved with an aggressive line of questioning that may imply that you are intentionally hiding something or you are biased.

If you see this happen, do not lose your temper or take the attack personally. You were calm and cool during direct questioning and you need to maintain that composure. Do not let the jury think you have some sort of split personality. If opposing counsel is really being a jerk, the jury will pick up on it.

If this type of situation arises, do not act defensive or become evasive in your answers. Listen to the question, take time to think about the answer, and then calmly answer the question.

Question Does Not Make Sense

During cross-examination, opposing counsel may ask a question that does not make any sense or struggle to ask the question correctly. Just be aware that this may be a simple tactic to get you to help him. If a question does not make sense and cannot be answered, just say so.

> **Q:** Let's talk about Windows and I want to ask you a hypothetical question.
>
> **A:** Which version of Windows do you want to talk about?
>
> **Q:** I want to talk about the system that was in place on this computer that you analyzed.

A: Okay.

Q: It was Windows; right?

A: Yes, it was Windows XP, but you said you were going to ask me a hypothetical; so I'm trying to follow along.

Q: Okay. A person has Windows XP. They open a program -- strike that. A person has Windows XP. They copy a program. Without opening it, does it change the access information?

A: I don't understand the question.

Opposing counsel was probably trying to ask a question about copying a file (not a program) and the effect that may have on the last accessed date and time stamp. It is not your role to assume what he may be asking you. Simply state you do not understand the question and let him clarify the question.

Misstating Your Testimony

During your cross-examination, opposing counsel may try mischaracterize your earlier testimony. You know what you said and now opposing counsel is trying to rephrase and change what you said. A red flag should go up when you hear, "*earlier you testified that...*" At this point, you should be listening closely for any subtle changes to your testimony.

Your counsel should object and the judge should admonish opposing counsel. However, what happens if the judge allows it? Here is an example:

Q: Well, on direct examination you said that Mr. Jones selected all of these options because he was trying to do X, Y, and Z to hide his tracks.

COUNSEL: Objection. Misstates the witness's testimony.

COURT: Overruled, you may proceed.

A: That is not what I said. What I said was the basic options were displayed in the demonstrative exhibit. The user can change the options at any time. In fact, the actual settings in the software on the defendant's computer were different and were set to exclude specific websites from deletion.

In this example, the judge allowed the question. Just provide a clear answer and restate your testimony.

Changing Your Opinion

During your cross-examination, opposing counsel may pose some type of question to see if you would change your opinion based on additional facts or assumptions. Opposing counsel may be trying to have you appear as unbending or prejudiced.

How do you deal with this type of questioning? You are not biased and your role as a computer forensic examiner is to be objective. You are always willing to look at any and all new information or facts and consider them. However, new information or facts may not cause you to change your opinion. Your opinion was based on the current facts in the case.

Opposing counsel may just come straight out and ask you what type of information would get you to change your opinion. The best way to deal with this type of question is the same way. You are always willing to look at any and all facts and consider changing your opinion if the new information supported it.

Opinion Formed

Opposing counsel may attempt to pin you down on when you formed your expert opinions. The objective may be to show that you formed your opinions prior to completing your analysis, which means you were not being objective. Opposing counsel may try to paint a picture to the jury that you only found evidence that supported the government's case and your opinion was formed at the very beginning of the investigation.

The report writing methodology described in this handbook is that your opinions are formed at the conclusion of your analysis. You were objective from the beginning of your analysis and your opinions were based on supporting facts. If you found exculpatory evidence or evidence that suggested a different opinion, then that information would have been presented in your report.

"I Don't Know"

If you do not know the answer to opposing counsel's question, do not be afraid to respond with, *"I don't know."* Sometimes people think that they have to know the answer to everything and that is just not possible. If you provide an answer only for appearance purposes, it could easily backfire as you are asked a longer series of questions based on your answer.

I once heard someone say that they like to include lots of "extra" (also known as superfluous) information attached to their report just in case someone asks them a question on the stand. He wanted to be able to look up the answer. First of all, you cannot possibly include every piece of information from a hard drive in your report. Second, who is asking you the question? Opposing counsel? If you do not know the answer, just say so. As I mentioned earlier, opposing counsel may be trying to use you as their expert to introduce evidence. If you honestly cannot answer the question, they may need to put their expert on the stand to testify.

The other downside to attaching superfluous information is you better be prepared to answer every single thing listed in those attachments. Opposing counsel could challenge you on that information in an effort to discredit you. If you were asked about some obscure registry information you included in your report, you will look silly to the jury when your answer is *"I don't know."* The simple follow-up responses from counsel will be something to the effect of, "this is your report, correct? As you sit here now, are you claiming not to understand your own report?"

Numbers

During your cross-examination, you may be asked to provide a number or a percentage. Unless this was something you documented in your report, you probably will not know the answer.

> **Q:** Did you do an analysis to determine, based on your opinion, what percentage was erotica and what percentage was pornography?

If you happen to know the answer, then provide the number to counsel. However, never guess or speculate if you do not know. This falls in line with the last section ("I Don't Know").

Interrupting Your Answers

There may be times when you are questioned during cross-examination and counsel does not like your answer or that you are trying to explain your answer. At this point, counsel may try to interrupt you.

> **Q:** Did you find any evidence of any types of time or clock-changing programs on defendant's computer media?
>
> **A:** No. Actually, sometimes when people have tried using software that specifically alters date and time stamps, there are --
>
> **Q:** One more question. With respect to the BXX.zip file, in your report you didn't find evidence that it had been unpacked.
>
> **A:** Counselor, you did not let me complete my answer to your prior question. May I complete my answer?
>
> **Q:** Go ahead.

In this example, the expert asked if he could complete his answer before answering the next question.

Learned Treatise

During your cross-examination, opposing counsel may hold up a particular textbook and ask you if you are familiar with it. Counsel may be setting the stage to introduce text from a learned treatise, which is an authoritative publication. For example, in a DNA case, the publication *Forensic DNA Typing, Second Edition: Biology, Technology, and Genetics of STR Markers* is considered authoritative in that field. In your case, opposing counsel may refer to a particular computer forensic manual.

> **Q:** You've talked about your background and training and expertise; correct?
>
> **A:** Yes.
>
> **Q:** You indicated that you are a certified forensic examiner for EnCase?
>
> **A:** Yes.
>
> **Q:** Are you familiar with the EnCase certified examiner manual?
>
> **A:** Yes.

Q: You've read that?

A: No.

Opposing counsel may reference the publication to do one of the following:

1) Have you admit the text within the publication is authoritative.

2) Have you admit you used portions of the publication to reach your conclusions.

If you happen to own a particular textbook, you may have it because one or two chapters provide some good reference material. While portions of the book may have good references, that does not mean the entire publication or even certain portions of it should be considered authoritative. You may know that there are technical errors within the book. If you were to agree that the entire textbook was authoritative, it will be difficult for you to disagree with text that opposing counsel may read from it.

If opposing counsel begins to cite text from the publication, he may ask you if you agree with it. Before you quickly answer the question, ask counsel for the specific page number and to physically hold the publication so you can read it yourself. Before you answer the question, you want to ensure the passage of text is not taken out of context or being misquoted. Take the time to read it and then properly answer the question.

While providing your answer, opposing counsel may interrupt you and try to force you into providing a simple "agree" or "disagree" answer. If you need to explain your answer, then let counsel know that you cannot give a simple answer. Simple answers can be misleading and you do not want the jury misled.

Final Remarks

You need to be well-prepared and know the details of your report. Part of being well-prepared is practicing how you will present information to the jury and knowing the tactics that opposing counsel may use to discredit your testimony.

Be professional and confident and the jury will respect your testimony. If opposing counsel is really being a jerk, then let him be the only jerk in the courtroom. From my experience, the jury will dislike his demeanor and may even let him know that they did not appreciate his attacks at the conclusion of the trial.

Appendix A:
Sample Reports

This section contains four sample reports with redacted exhibits. These sample reports are provided as guides to offer examples for organizing and formatting your forensic reports.

Report #1

Summary

I have conducted a computer forensic examination of the hard drive contained within the defendant's computer, which was seized pursuant to a search warrant. Based on my analysis, I found that the computer had been used to intentionally download digital photographs and videos depicting child pornography using peer-to-peer software. Additionally, I found that the computer had been used to intentionally download digital photographs depicting child pornography from a Russian photo sharing website.

Introduction

On June 15, 2012, I was requested to conduct a computer forensic examination of a Hewlett Packard (HP) netbook computer that was seized pursuant to a search warrant dated June 12, 2012. The defendant associated with the search warrant was involved in an undercover peer-to-peer child pornography investigation conducted by a federal law enforcement agency. The scope of my analysis was to review the defendant's hard drive and provide a written report of my findings.

List of Data Reviewed and Methodology

My analysis and report is based, in part, on my education, training, and experience in the field of computer forensics and law enforcement.

I have read the initial report documenting the undercover investigation and the search warrant dated June 12, 2012.

On June 15, 2012, I received the defendant's HP netbook computer (model Mini 110, serial number ABC12345). This computer contained a Seagate 160 GB SATA hard drive, serial number 1ZY1234X.

I created a forensic image of the 160 GB hard drive using a Tableau T35es write-block device and EnCase version 6.19. The image was successfully created with zero errors.

I examined the forensic image using EnCase Forensic Edition (version 6.19.4), which is a commercially available program.

At the start and conclusion of my analysis, I verified the MD5 hash value for the forensic image (ABC80097BC008570D5F9CA65BDB10B40) and zero errors were detected.

During my analysis, I used VMware (version 8.04), which is a commercially available program, to run the forensic image of the hard drive in a virtual environment. This environment allowed me to use the operating system and installed software in the same manner as it would appear on the HP computer. Using this environment, I was able to create screenshots to demonstrate activity as it would have appeared on the actual computer.

During my analysis, I extracted data from the Windows Volume Shadow Copy files by mounting the forensic image as a physical disk and using the dd imaging utility from the Forensic Acquisition Utilities (build 1.3.0.2390) distributed by GMG Systems, Inc. This utility is a publically available program.

Summary of Opinions

Opinion 1

The defendant's computer was running peer-to-peer software, which was used to intentionally download digital photographs and movies that depicted child pornography from other computers on the Internet. While the movies were being downloaded, the user previewed portions of those movies and then allowed to the movies to complete the download process.

Opinion 2

The defendant's computer was used to create a user account for a Russian website that is maintained for the purpose of hosting and sharing digital photographs. Personal photographs of the defendant along with photographs of children taken during the 2012 Rose Parade were uploaded to the website and associated those images with this user account. The website was searched with words associated with children and nudity. Digital photographs depicting child pornography and child erotica were intentionally downloaded from this website and stored in a

specific user-created folder that would allow the peer-to-peer software to share those images with other people on the Internet.

Detailed Analysis

The defendant's computer had Windows 7 Starter Edition installed as the operating system. When first prompted to create a new user account, the username of "temp" was used on 12/1/2009. That username was later modified to "Omar the Horrible." However, since the username was first called "temp," a user profile named "temp" was created and files associated with that profile were stored in C:\Users\temp.

The Guest account was enabled on 9/18/2010 and last used on 9/20/2010. The Guest account does not have access to the temp account or files within the temp profile.

The temp account (aka "Omar the Horrible") was password-protected. The Windows login screen is attached as Exhibit A.

Once logged in as "Omar the Horrible," the user's desktop appeared, which is attached as Exhibit B.

Using Windows Explorer to display the user's Pictures folder (My Pictures), you can see a user-created hidden folder called ptxxx, which is attached as Exhibit C. The ability to see this hidden folder (depicted as a faded folder icon) was enabled by the user through a setting in Windows Explorer.

The ptxxx folder contains other subfolders, such as my lil ones, img, vid, 2012 parade kids, gif, and Incomplete (see Exhibit C, page 2).

MP3 Rocket

MP3 Rocket is a peer-to-peer file sharing program. Version 5.4.7 was the current version installed on the defendant's hard drive.

MP3 Rocket was not configured to auto-start when the user logged in and required the user to manual start the program to run it.

This version of MP3 Rocket has the same functionality of an open-source peer-to-peer program known as Limewire. In testing this version of the software in a

controlled environment, I found it to function the same way as Limewire in the way that you could search, download, preview downloads in progress, view completed downloads, and configure the program.

When MP3 Rocket is first installed, it creates one folder for downloading files (Incomplete) and one folder for sharing files (Shared). When a user selects a file to download, a temporary file is created in the Incomplete folder. The temporary file is given a prefix to the original file name. The prefix consists of the letter T and a number, which is the file size (total number of bytes or characters within the file) An example would be "T-20265280-The Lord of the Rings – The Hobbit 2006 Trailer.mpeg."

Once the file has completed downloading, the filename prefix is removed and it is moved from the Incomplete folder and stored in the Shared folder.

The user has the ability to define specific folders that completed downloads can be stored based on media type. In this case, the user defined specific folders for images and videos:

C:\Users\temp\Pictures\ptxxx\img

C:\Users\temp\Pictures\ptxxx\vid

A screenshot showing the user settings is displayed in Exhibit D, page 1.

When the user makes this change, the user is then prompted to share these new folders. The prompt the user would see is displayed in Exhibit D, page 2.

The user has the option to share or not share these folders. On the defendant's computer, the user clicked OK to add these folders to be shared. A screenshot showing the settings for Shared Folders is displayed in Exhibit D, page 3.

To provide a simple depiction of the running software, I created screenshots of MP3 Rocket. These screenshots are attached as Exhibit E.

Exhibit E, Page 1, shows the Search Tab for All Types of files. From this tab, the user could select a specific file type that he was interested in finding (such as an image or video) and then type a search term(s). This also shows the incomplete files that had been selected for download, but have not finished downloading.

During the download, the user has the option to preview the file before the file has completed downloading. For example, if a video file was 22% complete, the user would click on the Preview button. The software creates a copy of the in-progress download and adds the prefix of "**Preview-**" to the filename. This allows the user to watch the partially downloaded video file, while the remainder of the video continues to download.

Exhibit E, Page 2, shows the My Files Tab and a partial listing of the files stored in the shared folder named "img."

Exhibit E, Page 3, shows the My Files Tab and a partial listing of the files stored in the shared folder named "vid."

Download Activity

Typically, files that exist in the user's P2P shared folder originated from one of two activities:

1) The user downloaded the file using peer-to-peer software from others across the Internet.

2) The user copied the file from his personal collection of data.

Understanding the process of how files are retrieved from other users across the Internet using MP3 Rocket and what artifacts are created from that activity will help to establish evidence of downloading.

Files that are being downloaded with MP3 Rocket are given a temporary filename, which consists of a prefix (T-########-) and the original filename. These files are stored in the Incomplete directory.

Individual entries for each incomplete file, including the hash value, are listed within a file named "downloads.dat," which is a file maintained by MP3 Rocket. The downloads.dat file is constantly being updated while MP3 Rocket is running and downloading files.

The file creation time of the file being downloaded is the time that the file was selected by the user to be downloaded. As blocks of blocks of data are downloaded and added to that file, the last written time of the file is updated.

Once the download is complete, the file is renamed by MP3 Rocket to its original filename and moved to the designated Shared directory. The last written time of the file is when the file finished downloading.

The Downloads.dat file in this version of MP3 Rocket also stores the user's search terms. In this case, the downloads.dat file contained the following user search terms:

> 9yo
>
> pthc black
>
> pedo dad

The user also searched specifically for videos using MP3 Rocket using the following 8 search terms:

> 9yo
>
> pthc black
>
> 8yo
>
> toddler
>
> 3yo toddler girl
>
> pedo dad
>
> 2yo
>
> pthc family

A file listing of the Incomplete folder (C:\Users\temp\Incomplete) is attached as Exhibit F. The file created time of the file is when the user selected the file to be downloaded using MP3 Rocket. The last written time is the last time a block of data associated with the file had been downloaded.

A file listing of the vid folder (C:\Users\temp\pictures\ptxxx\vid) is attached as Exhibit G. This folder contained 158 digital movies of which 150 depict child pornography.

A file listing of the img folder (C:\Users\temp\pictures\ptxxx\img) is attached as Exhibit H. This folder contained 824 digital photographs of which 800 depict child pornography and child erotica. It should be noted that not all of the photographs contained in this folder were downloaded using MP3 Rocket.

Volume Shadow Copy

Windows 7 runs a service known as Volume Shadow Copy, which makes a differential backup of the data on a volume, which includes user-created files. Shadow copies of data can provide a time capsule view of a volume at a particular time, which can be used to demonstrate how files have been altered or deleted. In reviewing this service, I found that the service created backups at the following dates and times:

12/26/11 02:02:17 PM (MP3 Rocket activity)

12/30/11 02:48:03 AM

01/02/12 01:52:05 PM

01/02/12 03:23:13 PM

01/02/12 03:50:40 PM

01/06/12 12:15:38 PM (MP3 Rocket activity)

01/06/12 04:00:16 PM

01/10/12 11:19:59 AM

01/11/12 04:53:20 PM

01/16/12 03:09:35 PM (MP3 Rocket activity)

01/19/12 06:50:53 PM

01/22/12 07:40:35 PM

01/25/12 03:36:56 PM (MP3 Rocket activity)

01/29/12 05:42:39 PM

02/01/12 11:39:38 PM (MP3 Rocket activity)

I reviewed each backup that may have captured any activity associated with MP3 Rocket and noted it in the above list. After that review, I restored the data from those dates and conducted further analysis.

From the restored volume shadow copy backup dated 12/26/2011, I could see the user's P2P download activity in the Incomplete folder. Based on the activity in that folder, I could see the user actively downloading files and previewing downloads-in-progress (see Exhibit I).

From the restored volume shadow copy backup dated 1/6/2012, I could see new user P2P activity in the Incomplete folder. Exhibit J displays the folder activity.

In Exhibits I and J, I found examples of previewed downloads-in-progress where the downloads were allowed to continue until completion (these items were highlighted in the exhibits). The completed files were located in the current vid folder (C:\Users\temp\pictures\ptxxx\vid). By using the information from the restored volume shadow copy backup data (specifically Exhibits I and J), I was able to create a timeline that demonstrates the following activity for 16 digital movies that depict child pornography:

1. When the user selected the file for download

2. When the user previewed the file while the download was in progress

3. When the download completed

This timeline is represented in Exhibit K.

IMGSRC.RU Website

As stated earlier, not all of the photographs contained in the img folder (C:\Users\temp\pictures\ptxxx\img) were downloaded using MP3 Rocket. Based on the file naming convention, and the date/time stamps, it appeared that the files had been copied directly from a website.

By conducting a search of the user's Internet Explorer cached data for filenames found in the img folder, I found evidence that the files came from a website with the URL of http://imgsrc.ru. I am familiar with this specific website. This website offers a free service as a digital photo hosting service, which is located in Russia. The site allows people to search the "photo albums" of other users and post digital photos of their own. In order to post pictures, a user must register with a valid email address. After completing the basic registration information, the site sends an email containing the login password to the user.

By searching the user's cached Internet Explorer data, I found that the user created an account using the email address of [redacted]@hotmail.com. I found cached webpages that matched the live website page for the user's profile. A copy of the live webpage is attached as Exhibit L.

Both the live webpage and the cached page shows the user account of [*redacted*] was created on 2/4/2011 and the user info states "*guy with nice body looking to make video with girls or boys 6-12 email me with pics of your girl or boy*"

The user created two online photo albums at the site with the following descriptions:

1. "cropped nude pics of myself (eze) (password protected)," which was created on 1/23/2012.

2. "sexy kids at a parade (no nude)," which was created on 1/23/2012.

The first album matched images found on the hard drive in the user's profile in the following folder: C:\Users\temp\Pictures\my icon pix. This folder contains additional photos of the defendant.

The second album matched images found on the hard drive in the user's profile in the following folder: C:\Users\temp\Pictures\ptxxx\2012 parade kids. This folder contains 25 digital photos, which were taken on 1/2/2012 at the Rose Parade and copied to the computer on 1/2/2012. This set of 25 photos were extracted from a larger set of 171 photos taken at the parade using a SONY·DSC-T300 camera, which were in the following folder: C:\Users\temp\Pictures\ 2012 Rose Parade.

To search the website, a person can enter search terms and limit the results to a specific section, such as travel, family, and hobby. By searching the user's cache and HTML code found in unallocated space of the hard drive, I found that the user had been searching the website for photo albums using the following search terms and criteria:

kids (in section) nudity

boys (in section) nudity

girls (in section) nudity

naked (in section) kids

natural (in section) kids

bath (in section) kids

An example of a HTML search page found in the user's cache folder (C:\Users\temp\AppData\Local\Microsoft\Windows\Temporary Internet Files\Low \Content.IE5\7DYJ9765\search[1].htm) is attached as Exhibit M.

The cached web pages found on the hard drive indicated that the user was logged into the website (see Exhibit M as an example). In order to log in, you have to use a password which is sent to your registered email address.

The user then previewed photo albums based on the search criteria and saved specific photos to the img folder using the right-click, *Save picture as...* function of Internet Explorer.

It should be noted that not all of the user's Internet activity could be reported since Internet Explorer had been configured to *Delete browsing history on exit.*

Malware Detection

Microsoft Security Essentials was installed and functioning on the defendant's computer. There were no "harmful" items detected or listed. The software was up-to-date as of 2/1/2012 (virus and spyware definition version 1.119.1184.0 installed).

I conducted a separate virus scan of the hard drive using ESET NOD32 Antivirus (version 3.0.695.0, virus signature database 6872). The results of this scan identified no viruses or malware.

Exhibits

This report contains the following exhibits:

Exhibit A	Windows login screen
Exhibit B	User's desktop
Exhibit C	Windows Explorer, Pictures folder
Exhibit D	MP3 Rocket – Options
Exhibit E	MP3 Rocket – User Interface
Exhibit F	Incomplete folder file listing
Exhibit G	vid folder file listing
Exhibit H	img folder file listing
Exhibit I	Incomplete folder file listing from backup dated 12/26/2011
Exhibit J	Incomplete folder file listing from backup dated 1/6/2012
Exhibit K	Timeline of download and preview activity for specific videos
Exhibit L	Screenshot of live website imgsrc.ru matching cached page found on hard drive
Exhibit M	Cached user profile web page
Exhibit N	Cached search web page

EXHIBIT A

EXHIBIT B

EXHIBIT C

EXHIBIT C

EXHIBIT D

EXHIBIT D

EXHIBIT D

EXHIBIT E

EXHIBIT E

EXHIBIT E

EXHIBIT F

Name	File Created	Last Written	Logical Size
[filename redacted — describes child sexual abuse material]	12/1/11 11:41 AM	1/30/12 5:09 PM	315,545,599
[filename redacted]	10/30/11 7:21 AM	1/30/12 5:05 PM	578,799,020
[filename redacted]	10/30/11 6:51 AM	1/24/12 10:37 AM	67,282,944
[filename redacted]	1/3/12 4:00 AM	1/3/12 12:16 PM	72,435,712
[filename redacted]	10/30/11 6:51 AM	12/20/11 5:27 PM	17,576,982
[filename redacted]	12/20/11 5:00 AM	12/20/11 7:17 AM	61,287,876
[filename redacted]	12/20/11 4:59 AM	12/20/11 7:14 AM	67,588,891
[filename redacted]	12/20/11 4:24 AM	12/20/11 4:24 AM	0
[filename redacted]	12/20/11 4:07 AM	12/20/11 4:07 AM	0
[filename redacted]	12/20/11 4:02 AM	12/20/11 4:05 AM	333,315
[filename redacted]	11/9/11 5:41 PM	12/9/11 4:44 AM	495,976,448
[filename redacted]	10/30/11 7:00 AM	12/3/11 11:10 AM	14,680,064
[filename redacted]	12/1/11 1:53 PM	12/1/11 1:53 PM	0
[filename redacted]	12/1/11 12:32 PM	12/1/11 12:32 PM	0
[filename redacted]	12/1/11 12:00 PM	12/1/11 12:00 PM	0
[filename redacted]	12/1/11 11:59 AM	12/1/11 11:59 AM	0
[filename redacted]	12/1/11 11:58 AM	12/1/11 11:58 AM	0
[filename redacted]	12/1/11 11:58 AM	12/1/11 11:58 AM	0
[filename redacted]	12/1/11 11:37 AM	12/1/11 11:37 AM	0
[filename redacted]	12/1/11 11:37 AM	12/1/11 11:37 AM	0
[filename redacted]	12/1/11 11:37 AM	12/1/11 11:37 AM	0

EXHIBIT G



Name	File Created	Last Written	Logical Size
[redacted]	1/3/12 4:09 AM	1/30/12 10:18 AM	93,548,639
[redacted]	12/20/11 4:28 AM	1/13/12 5:30 AM	26,674,460
[redacted]	1/3/12 3:45 AM	1/3/12 7:43 AM	158,501,376
[redacted]	1/3/12 7:22 AM	1/3/12 7:22 AM	241,268,384
[redacted]	1/3/12 4:00 AM	1/3/12 4:26 AM	4,526,840
[redacted]	11/12/11 8:28 PM	1/3/12 4:06 AM	1,681,920
[redacted]	12/20/11 4:59 AM	12/20/11 5:09 AM	1,171,456
[redacted]	12/20/11 4:27 AM	12/20/11 4:54 AM	2,965,854
[redacted]	12/20/11 4:12 AM	12/20/11 4:39 AM	5,989,981
[redacted]	12/20/11 4:14 AM	12/20/11 4:19 AM	861,620
[redacted]	12/3/11 5:15 AM	12/3/11 5:19 AM	4,261,892
[redacted]	12/1/11 11:47 AM	12/1/11 6:15 PM	15,979,228
[redacted]	12/1/11 11:48 AM	12/1/11 1:13 PM	13,286,248
[redacted]	12/1/11 11:36 AM	12/1/11 12:53 PM	7,758,000
[redacted]	12/1/11 12:10 PM	12/1/11 12:10 PM	12,527,616
[redacted]	12/1/11 12:06 PM	12/1/11 12:06 PM	31,012,338
[redacted]	12/1/11 11:15 AM	12/1/11 11:29 AM	19,466,522
[redacted]	11/12/11 8:17 PM	12/1/11 11:15 AM	15,345,626
[redacted]	11/12/11 8:18 PM	12/1/11 4:34 AM	9,395,708
[redacted]	11/14/11 6:33 PM	11/14/11 6:36 PM	2,149,396
[redacted]	[illegible]	[illegible]	7,413,845
[redacted]	3/1/11 3:29 AM	3/1/11 3:29 AM	83,[illegible]
[redacted]	3/1/11 3:07 AM	3/1/11 3:10 AM	1,157,554
[redacted]	3/1/11 2:57 AM	3/1/11 2:57 AM	7,546,880
[redacted]	3/1/11 2:40 AM	3/1/11 2:46 AM	14,596,096
[redacted]	3/1/11 2:17 AM	3/1/11 2:43 AM	1,192,243
[redacted]	3/1/11 2:12 AM	3/1/11 2:12 AM	47,400,964

EXHIBIT H

Name	File Created	Last Written	Logical Size
26744484DIu.jpg	1/31/12 7:17 PM	1/31/12 7:17 PM	91,676
26744481PLL.jpg	1/31/12 7:16 PM	1/31/12 7:16 PM	167,712
26697060Cyj.jpg	1/31/12 7:00 PM	1/31/12 7:00 PM	75,689
26645670ToD.jpg	1/31/12 6:56 PM	1/31/12 6:56 PM	111,802
26222555ajN.jpg	1/31/12 6:55 PM	1/31/12 6:55 PM	136,194
26080554gZj.jpg	1/31/12 6:54 PM	1/31/12 6:54 PM	229,656
26777018jcp.jpg	1/31/12 6:34 PM	1/31/12 6:34 PM	84,990
26777014zxD.jpg	1/31/12 6:33 PM	1/31/12 6:32 PM	144,999
26861490pjE.jpg	1/31/12 6:27 PM	1/31/12 6:27 PM	79,977
26861483fnJ.jpg	1/31/12 6:27 PM	1/31/12 6:27 PM	65,230
26862752iCu.jpg	1/31/12 6:25 PM	1/31/12 6:25 PM	68,654
26862690QbN.jpg	1/31/12 6:25 PM	1/31/12 6:24 PM	118,979
26765409lbh.jpg	1/31/12 6:21 PM	1/31/12 6:21 PM	74,364
26722487PGh.jpg	1/31/12 6:20 PM	1/31/12 6:20 PM	107,119
26722461ICl.jpg	1/31/12 6:20 PM	1/31/12 6:20 PM	139,550
26848900PMI.jpg	1/31/12 6:14 PM	1/31/12 6:14 PM	58,439
26848896Ujn.jpg	1/31/12 6:13 PM	1/31/12 6:13 PM	29,506
26807050sKB.jpg	1/30/12 4:35 AM	1/30/12 4:35 AM	114,315
26527615Lao.jpg	1/22/12 9:51 PM	1/22/12 9:51 PM	83,400
26522557GdV.jpg	1/22/12 9:40 PM	1/22/12 9:40 PM	27,793
26568755MYA.jpg	1/13/12 4:05 AM	1/13/12 4:05 AM	59,635
26558873ZDM.jpg	1/13/12 3:33 AM	1/13/12 3:33 AM	83,968
26343766JhG.jpg	1/13/12 3:24 AM	1/13/12 3:23 AM	67,235
pictures from ranchi torpedo dloaded in 2009- pedo kdv kidzilla pthc toddlers 0yo 1yo 2yo 3yo 4yo 5yo 6yo 9yo _____ (26).jpg	10/16/11 6:37 AM	10/18/11 5:05 AM	27,840
PTHC Pedo NEW Childporn Private Daughter Girl_126241588439 8.jpg	10/16/11 6:27 AM	10/18/11 4:45 AM	177,933
pictures from ranchi torpedo dloaded in 2009- pedo kdv kidzilla pthc toddlers 0yo 1yo 2yo 3yo 4yo 5yo 6yo 9yo tar.jpg	10/16/11 6:25 AM	10/18/11 4:20 AM	233,283
PTHC Pedo NEW Childporn Private Daughter Girl_126241453419 4.jpg	10/16/11 6:26 AM	10/18/11 4:20 AM	203,534
PTHC Pedo NEW Childporn Private Daughter 54584_12376894794 75_123_1002lo.jpg	10/16/11 6:25 AM	10/18/11 4:10 AM	123,841

EXHIBIT I

Name	File Created	Last Written	Logical Size
T-17576982-Excellent.avi	10/30/11 6:51 AM	12/20/11 5:27 PM	17,576,982
Preview-T-61287876-Pedo - Pthc - [redacted] And Man 2007 - Se-(1).avi		12/20/11 7:17 AM	1,100,665
T-61287876-Pedo - Pthc - [redacted] And Man 2007 -Se-(1).avi	12/20/11 5:00 AM	12/20/11 7:17 AM	61,287,876
T-67588892-(Pthc) 4Yo Daughter's [redacted].mpg	12/20/11 4:59 AM	12/20/11 7:14 AM	67,588,891
Preview-T-17576982-Excellent.avi	12/20/11 5:33 AM	12/20/11 5:33 AM	3,906,068
Preview-T-207710861-Pedo Mom & Dad [redacted] (Pthc - 20m15S)(1).mpg	12/20/11 5:33 AM	12/20/11 5:33 AM	23,696,759
Preview-T-33308160-Bibcam - 11Yo Witty-Full.avi	12/20/11 5:12 AM	12/20/11 5:33 AM	7,340,031
Preview-T-67588892-(Pthc) 4Yo Daughter's [redacted].mpg	12/20/11 5:32 AM	12/20/11 5:32 AM	13,369,343
T-26674460-(Pthc) - 2008 - [redacted] 10Yr wichst Papa.avi	12/20/11 4:28 AM	12/20/11 5:30 AM	24,903,680
T-10709068-(Pthc) (Ptsc) Bibcam - 10Yo [redacted].avi	12/20/11 4:27 AM	12/20/11 5:30 AM	10,709,068
T-74466-mom.and.son.mutter.und.sohn.geile [redacted] mom.jung.boy.older.woman-by [redacted] JPG	12/20/11 5:07 AM	12/20/11 5:20 AM	65,507
T-49062-mom.and.son.mutter.und.sohn.geile [redacted] mom.jung.boy.older.woman-by [redacted] JPG	12/20/11 5:07 AM	12/20/11 5:07 AM	0
Preview-T-26674460-(Pthc) - 2008 - [redacted] 10Yr wichst Papa.avi	12/20/11 4:45 AM	12/20/11 4:45 AM	411,591
Preview-T-8433453-PTHC-kids in action-very hard!!.mpg	12/20/11 4:44 AM	12/20/11 4:44 AM	104,175
Preview-T-2965854-INew Pthc 0602 [redacted] 8Yo Pedo Ptsc.avi	12/20/11 4:33 AM	12/20/11 4:33 AM	111,454
Preview-T-13024904-7011 PTHC-girl 9yo [redacted] 5yo boys girls pedo 2011 NEW [redacted]	12/1/11 11:10 AM	12/20/11 4:32 AM	642,013
T-106520-REAL & Photo by [redacted] Preteen [redacted], pedo, boys and girls [redacted], teens, young, family, taboo, webcam, [redacted] virgin, virgins, schoolteens.net, [redacted] 12yo.jpg	6/8/10 3:38 AM	6/8/10 3:38 AM	0
T-128238-SICK 2 tiny [redacted] 3 year old 4 5 6 7 8 9 10 11 12 13 14 yo kiddie paido pedo child children boy [redacted] porn porno [redacted].jpg	6/8/10 3:38 AM	6/8/10 3:38 AM	0
T-36499-INNOCENTLY Children [redacted] !SUPER! child porn teen preteen underage Kindergarden pic IY! [redacted] Russian asia littlegirl boy 3yo 3yr pedo [redacted] ille.jpg	6/8/10 3:03 AM	6/8/10 3:03 AM	0

EXHIBIT J

Name	File Created	Last Written	Logical Size
T-72435712-(pthc) (12yo) On Divider Ready For .avi	1/3/12 4:00 AM	1/3/12 12:16 PM	72,435,712
Preview-T-158501376-Pedoland 10Yr in Yellow Dress Day01 ((kingpass)) (Pthc).avi	1/3/12 3:58 AM	1/3/12 4:46 AM	23,954,866
Preview-T-241268384-XXX Real Pedo Porn (pthc Frifam Pedoland) A0309.mpg	1/3/12 4:40 AM	1/3/12 4:40 AM	28,599,671
T-93548639-Pthc-Pedoland-Frifam-2010-9Yo- -Compil-v2.mpg	1/3/12 4:09 AM	1/3/12 4:09 AM	0
Preview-T-42658768-(Pthc) - 8m39S.avi	1/3/12 4:05 AM	1/3/12 4:09 AM	1,225,129
Preview-T-4526840-pthc hussyfan(PT) _h.mpg	1/3/12 4:03 AM	1/3/12 4:08 AM	1,069,492
Preview-T-72435712-(pthc) (12yo) On Divider Ready For .avi	1/3/12 4:08 AM	1/3/12 4:08 AM	975,753
Preview-T-49875115-P101- 5yo Boy + friend .mpg	1/3/12 3:57 AM	1/3/12 4:05 AM	4,287,215
Preview-T-47360000-pthc Pedoland Frifam Georgia Peach - Tent2 (2006).avi	1/3/12 3:58 AM	1/3/12 4:03 AM	4,009,620
Preview-T-26057356-(pthc PedoFamily 01 - (2011).AVI	1/3/12 3:48 AM	1/3/12 3:58 AM	2,512,760
Preview-T-26057356-(pthc PedoFamily 01 - (2011).AVI	1/3/12 3:50 AM	1/3/12 3:58 AM	2,393,975
T-184019652-(Pthc Frifam Pedoland) Hot Privat XXX Porn Movies Collection - 27.mpg	1/3/12 3:53 AM	1/3/12 3:57 AM	15,372,288
Preview-T-184019652-(Pthc Frifam Pedoland) Hot Privat XXX Porn Movies Collection - 27.mpg	1/3/12 3:57 AM	1/3/12 3:57 AM	4,526,792
Preview-T-82128400-(pthc) 13Yo Boy 10Yo Brazil.mpg	1/3/12 3:51 AM	1/3/12 3:51 AM	2,919,365

EXHIBIT K

Name	Download Start	Previewed	Download Finish
2010 Pthc Pedo Frifam ▨▨▨ Film2.mpg	11/9/11 6:00 PM	11/10/11 11:40 AM	11/13/11 4:18 AM
Pedo - Pthc - (New) Kid Cam ▨▨▨ mpg	11/12/11 8:06 PM	11/12/11 8:11 PM	11/12/11 8:19 PM
(Pthc) ▨▨▨ 7Yo - ▨▨▨▨▨▨▨▨▨▨ -Sound,Divx & Wmp- (Map).avi	11/12/11 8:17 PM	11/14/11 4:19 PM	12/1/11 11:15 AM
PTHC - 12YO reverse cowgirl.mpg	11/12/11 8:23 PM	11/12/11 8:47 PM	11/12/11 9:02 PM
PTHC -B- man&boy 11yo ▨▨▨▨▨.avi	11/14/11 4:23 PM	11/14/11 4:29 PM	11/14/11 4:46 PM
▨▨▨ girl - Pthc ▨▨▨▨▨▨▨.mpg	12/1/11 11:15 AM	12/1/11 11:27 AM	12/1/11 11:29 AM
A Family ▨▨▨▨▨▨▨▨▨▨▨▨▨ Kiddie's, They	12/1/11 11:47 AM	12/1/11 4:29 PM	12/1/11 6:15 PM
Child ▨▨▨▨▨▨▨ (1m30s) Xxx Pthc.mpg			
(Pthc) ▨▨▨▨ 5Yo - ▨▨▨▨▨.mpg	12/3/11 5:15 AM	12/1/11 11:01 AM	12/3/11 5:19 AM
!!NEW!! ▨▨▨ 3yo 5yo 7yo__ ▨▨▨▨▨▨▨▨▨▨▨▨▨▨▨ KOOL	12/20/11 4:12 AM	12/20/11 4:13 AM	12/20/11 4:39 AM
ptsc pthc.mpg			
PRETEEN - KDV - RBV - ▨▨▨▨▨▨▨ - BOY - pedo 10 anos ▨▨▨.avi	12/20/11 4:14 AM	12/20/11 4:15 AM	12/20/11 4:19 AM
!New Pthc 06O2 ▨▨▨▨▨ 8Yo Pedo Pthc.avi	12/20/11 4:27 AM	12/20/11 4:33 AM	12/20/11 4:54 AM
(Pthc) - 2008 - ▨▨ 10Yr wichst Papa.avi	12/20/11 4:28 AM	12/20/11 4:45 AM	1/13/11 5:30 AM
Pedoland ▨▨▨ 10yr. In Yellow Dress Day01 ((Kingpass)) (Pthc).avi	1/3/12 3:45 AM	1/3/12 3:58 AM	1/3/12 7:43 AM
pthc hussyfan(PT) ;` ▨▨▨▨▨▨▨▨▨_h.mpg	1/3/12 4:00 AM	1/3/12 4:03 AM	1/3/12 4:26 AM
Pthc-Pedoland-Frifam-2010-9Yo- ▨▨▨-Compil-v2.mpg	1/3/12 4:09 AM	1/3/12 4:09 AM	1/30/12 10:18 AM
XXX Real Pedo Porn (pthc Frifam Pedoland) AO309.mpg	1/3/12 7:22 AM	1/3/12 4:40 AM	1/3/12 7:22 AM

EXHIBIT L

iMGSRC.RU albums of

login, upload your photos!

join free | search | more users | FAQ | русский

Email

Registered on: 2011-02-04

User info: black guy with nice body looking to make video with girls or boys 6-12 email me with pics of your girl or boy

Tagged under: african, black, bottoms, boy, cute, girls, kids, naked, nude, preteen, sexy, teen.

name ▲▼ (hide album previews)

name ▲▼	photos	in section ▲▼	pageviews*	comm	modified ▲▼
cropped nude pics of myself (eze) (password protected)	6	kids	0+11876	3	2012-01-23 09:16
sexy kids at a parade (no nude)	26	kids	92+364569	6	2012-01-23 09:02
Статистика показанных альбомов (2):	32		92+376445	9	

Create new album

iMGSRC.RU - FREE photo hosting since 2006. © iMGSRC.RU team. All photos are © their respective posters/owners. TOS/FAQ. Информация для родителей.

EXHIBIT M

iMGSRC.RU Album editor

Back to albums index

Привет, prefiend! All your albums are accessible via this link - http://prefiend.imgsrc.ru.

Hello, ▮▮▮ Your albums are here.

Logout.

join free|search|more users|FAQ|русский

Аватар:

[×]

Browse...

Çáåá-äôu

Your personal data:

Real name:
Email: hide: ☐
Homepage:
ICQ UIN:
Birthdate: 0000-00-00
User info: black guy with nice body
 looking to make video with

Save your personal info

Your password for albums edit:

Current password:
New password:
Confirm new password:

Submit changes

* This is NOT a password for viewing albums.
Keep it secret.
** 6 chars min

Create new album:

[☺] Rambler's Top100

EXHIBIT N

iMGSRC.RU. Album search. boys

Hello, ▮▮▮▮ Your albums are here. Logout

join free search more users FAQ русский

Album search:

boys [search]

w/o passwords ☐ in section: nudity

Search results for 'boys' in section 'nudity':

name (show album previews)	photos	in section	modified
grcc GO GO BOYS	41	nudity	2012-01-30 03:45
boyloverb Sexy Boys	11	nudity	2012-01-30 00:58
god_of_nature: boys & girls	50	nudity	2012-01-29 23:23
sickhealth: trading boys	20	nudity	2012-01-08 04:28
lostboardies_AB Karate_Sauna boys (password protected)	168	nudity	2012-01-08 03:01
skinboi110_19 willy and sonic cute teen boys shower	30	nudity	2012-01-07 01:45
colecolecole: Boysbutts	30	nudity	2012-01-06 13:06
microsizerrc: bibcam boys	10	nudity	2012-01-04 07:47

всего найдено альбомов: 1049, страницы (100 альбомов на странице): 1 2 3 4 5 6 7 8 9 10 11

NB: small albums and unmoderated content not shown. See FAQ.

iMGSRC.RU. FREE photo hosting since 2006. © Skinny Bravo & k8. All photos copyright by their respective posters/owners.

TOS FAQ родителям

Report #2

Summary

This report provides information associated with the hard drive installed in the defendant's personal computer and a rewritable optical disc that was found in the defendant's possession.

Based on my analysis, I found that the hard drive contained digital photographs depicting child pornography, which were taken with a Minolta DiMAGE S414 digital camera. Additionally, I recovered deleted digital photographs depicting child pornography from the rewritable optical disc, which were taken with the same make and model of digital camera.

List of Evidence Reviewed and Methodology

I reviewed the following items of evidence:

1) Forensic image of 40GB Maxtor hard drive from defendant's computer, which was created with Encase version 5.05e on September 19, 2006 at 12:21:14am. I verified the integrity of the Encase image and it verified with zero errors. The acquisition MD5 hash value matched the verification MD5 hash value (6ABC93AFB296757DED3E2E8433D52122).

2) Rewritable optical disc (CD-RW), hereafter referred to as CD1. This disc is labeled by the manufacturer as TDK CD-RW80. I created an ISO image of this disc using ISOBuster.

I examined the forensic image of the hard drive using EnCase Forensic Edition, which is a commercially available program.

During my analysis of CD1, I used ISOBuster and GetData's Recover My Files.

Detailed Analysis of 40GB Maxtor Drive

The 40GB Maxtor hard drive that was installed in the defendant's desktop computer was running Windows XP as the operating system. The operating system was installed on May 28, 2005 at 11:33am (UTC). The operating system had a user profile named Karl, which was created on May 28, 2005.

The time zone of the operating system was set to SE Asia Standard Time, which is GMT +7.

I found that a Minolta DIMAGE digital camera was first connected to a USB port on the desktop computer on June 4, 2005 at 15:48:39 (local time).

During my analysis of the 40GB Maxtor hard drive, I located files depicting child pornography in the following locations:

1. Nero PhotoShow Express album data

2. Windows Recycle Bin (Karl's user profile)

3. Norton Recycle Bin

PhotoShow Express

Nero PhotoShow Express is a program used to organize and manage digital photographs. The user interface is depicted in Exhibit A, Page 1.

PhotoShow Express was configured to detect a digital camera and removable media being attached to the computer. When the user attached a digital camera or removable media to the computer, PhotoShow Express would display a message to the user indicating that new pictures were found and prompt the user to add them to PhotoShow (see Exhibit A, Page 1).

The user would then select the digital photos and add them to a new album or an existing album on the computer.

If the user selects the default of creating a new album, the user is then prompted to name the new album (see Exhibit A, Page 2).

The user is then prompted to erase all of the digital photographs on the attached device after the album is created (see Exhibit A, Page 2).

At that point, the album creation process starts, which consists of two main functions:

1) The digital photographs are copied to the user's Windows profile, specifically the My Documents\My Pictures folder. A new subfolder is created based on the album name;

2) The program creates a thumbnail-sized image of each digital photograph. These thumbnail images are stored in a separate folder for each album and located in the user's Windows profile (Application Data\Ahead\PSD Image

Database\cache\albums). The naming convention for each album folder is based on an incremental number followed by an underscore and the name of the album. For example, "4_Matt's Party July 2005" is album number four and the album name is "Matt's Party July 2005."

Each album folder contains a file (album_info.txt) that provides information such as the album name, folder containing the digital photographs, and the name of each digital photograph.

Exhibit B lists all of the PhotoShow albums on the 40GB Maxtor hard drive including the date the album was created, and the path of the actual digital photographs.

For example, on February 25, 2006, at 10:20 a.m., a folder was created in Karl's user profile named My Documents\My Pictures\Matt and James. That folder contains 64 digital photographs taken with a Minolta DiMAGE S414 digital camera. At that same date and time, a PhotoShow album was created named Matt and James, which contains 64 matching thumbnail images of the digital photographs.

Exhibit B lists the status of the folder containing the digital photographs in Karl's user profile (My Documents\My Pictures). The status is either allocated (meaning the folder still exists) or missing (meaning that the folder had been deleted). Based on the evidence, it appears that the user deleted several folders containing digital photographs; however, the user maintained the matching PhotoShow album folders. I did not locate any images depicting child pornography in the allocated folders. However, I did locate thumbnail images of child pornography in the PhotoShow album folders, which is notated in Exhibit B.

Exhibit B also provides reference to the PhotoShow albums and CD1 in regards to digital photographs that were allocated on the CD and digital photographs that were recovered from unallocated space on the CD (see Detailed Analysis of Optical Media listed below).

Windows Recycle Bin

The Windows Recycle Bin associated with the user profile named Karl contained digital photographs depicting child pornography. These photographs were taken with a Minolta DiMAGE S414 digital camera.

The Windows XP operating system uses a separate "Recycle Bin" folder for each user account. The function of the Recycle Bin is to temporarily store files that have been intentionally deleted by the user so they can still be recovered if necessary.

By default, when a user deletes a file or an entire folder, the file or folder is moved to the user's Recycle Bin folder. The user has the option to restore the file back to the original location. The default storage capacity of the Recycle Bin is ten percent of the hard drive's capacity. If the amount of deleted files in the Recycle Bin exceeds that amount, then files are deleted from the Recycle Bin on a first-in, first-out basis. Although these files are considered to be permanently deleted from the user, they may still be recoverable from the hard drive using forensic software.

A user can access the Recycle Bin and intentionally delete individual items or all files and folders from the Recycle Bin.

In regards to the defendant's hard drive, the user's Recycle Bin had not been emptied since September 15, 2005.

A user can also intentionally delete files and folders and bypass the Recycle Bin function by using a keystroke combination of the [Shift]+[Delete] keys.

Norton Recycle Bin

The defendant's computer had Symantec's Norton SystemWorks 2005 installed. This program contains a feature called the Norton Protected Recycle Bin ("Norton Recycle Bin"), which resides within the Microsoft Windows Recycle Bin folder structure. The Norton Recycle Bin includes a hidden folder called NProtect.

The Norton Recycle Bin contained digital photographs depicting child pornography. These photographs were taken with a Minolta DiMAGE S414 digital camera.

Symantec's description of Norton Protection is as follows:

> *The Norton Protection feature protects many files from accidental deletion by making a temporary backup of the files at the time they are deleted, allowing you time to recover them if they were deleted by accident.*

> *Norton Protection acts a supplement to the Windows Recycle Bin, protecting many files that the Windows Recycle Bin does not protect. Norton Protection is not, however, a backup for the Windows Recycle Bin.*

Norton Protection is comprised of two features, the Norton Protected Recycle Bin and UnErase Wizard (also known as Norton UnErase). The Norton Protected Recycle Bin protects files by keeping a backup of deleted files. The UnErase Wizard recovers files from the Norton Protected Recycle Bin and the Windows Recycle Bin.

Digital Photograph Analysis

Digital cameras use a standard for the creating digital images. The image file format is known as exchangeable image file format (EXIF). In addition to the digital photograph itself, the EXIF image file also contains metadata, such as make and model of the camera, date and time information, camera settings, and a thumbnail-size image for previewing the photo.

During my analysis of the digital photographs taken with a Minolta DiMAGE S414 digital camera, I discovered that the date on the camera may not have been accurately set. It appeared that the date on the camera may have been off by approximately 185 days.

When I examined the defendant's computer, I found that the internal clock was accurate within 7 minutes:

System time: 12/13/07 07:51 a.m.

Actual time (PST): 12/12/07 16:58 p.m.

Since the actual camera was not available for examination, I conducted a date/time analysis based on the user's activity and user's descriptions of folder containing digital photos stored on the hard drive.

For example, there are 33 digital photographs stored in a folder called Girls 031606 (C:\Documents and Settings\Karl\My Documents\My Pictures\Girls 031606). Based on the folder naming convention, it appeared that the user was naming the folder with a description and a date. This specific folder was created on March 16, 2006. The digital photographs contain EXIF metadata indicating that the photos were taken on September 12, 2005 between 15:40 and 15:42. Based on this information, the camera appears to be off by -185 days.

I examined the digital photographs stored in a folder called Girls 031806. (C:\Documents and Settings\Karl\My Documents\My Pictures\Girls 031806). The

folder was created on March 18, 2006. The digital photographs contain EXIF metadata indicating that the photos were taken on September 13, 2005 and September 14, 2005.

Controlled Environment Analysis

Since the defendant's camera was not available for analysis, I purchased the same make and model of digital camera (Minolta DiMAGE S414) to conduct analysis in a controlled environment.

On February 17, 2008, I set the internal clock of the camera to August 16, 2006, which is -185 days. I inserted a Compact Flash memory card in the camera to store my photographs. I took 19 photographs on February 17, 2008 and an additional 3 photographs on February 19, 2008.

I restored the forensic image of the defendant's 40GB hard drive to a government-owned 40GB hard drive to create a working copy of the defendant's hard drive. I attached the restored hard drive to the defendant's computer and started the computer.

I connected the Compact Flash memory card to a USB port on the defendant's computer and Nero's PhotoShow Express automatically started when the memory card was detected. I was prompted to add the new photographs stored on the memory card to PhotoShow (see Exhibit C, Page 1).

I was then presented with thumbnail-sized images of each photograph with an option to add the photos to a new PhotoShow album (see Exhibit C, Page 1).

After I selected the default of adding all photos to a new album, I was prompted to enter the name of the new album (see Exhibit C, Page 2). In this example, I used the album name of "Ranch 021708," which is similar to the naming convention found on the defendant's computer, such as "Girls 031606."

As represented in the exhibit screenshot, the album date field was automatically populated with 8/16/2007. PhotoShow was pulling that date from the EXIF data found on the first photograph I took.

PhotoShow automatically created a folder named Ranch 021708 (C:\Documents and Settings\Karl\My Documents\My Pictures\Ranch 021708) and copied all of the photographs from the memory card to that folder. PhotoShow also created a separate album folder, which included a thumbnail image of each photograph (see Exhibit C, Page 3).

In the exhibit screenshot, the Album pane shows some of the other albums that existed on the defendant's computer. Next to each album name is the album date, which is the EXIF date extracted from the first photo in each album. This date is also listed in each album's info file (album_info.txt), which I referred to in my first report. The album_info.txt file contains information such as: album name; full path of the album photos; album date; and individual photo information (name, EXIF date, thumbnail image info, and resolution).

The exhibit screenshot also shows an offset between the user-named album and the album date.

Based on my findings in my controlled environment, I found consistent evidence to conclude that the date set on the camera used to create the photographs found on the defendant's hard drive (Minolta DiMAGE S414) was off by -185 days.

It should be noted that in addition to my analysis, additional evidence of the camera date offset can be found by using information stored in the PhotoShow album info files.

Deleted Photograph Analysis

When a user deletes an album within PhotoShow, the album folder, which is located in the user's Windows profile (Application Data\Ahead\PSD Image Database\cache\albums), is moved to a trash folder (Application Data\Ahead\PSD Image Database\cache\trash_albums). If the album is deleted, the actual digital photographs, which are stored in a subfolder in the user's My Pictures folder, are not deleted. Even if the user empties the trash within PhotoShow, the album folder information remains in the trash folder. The defendant's hard drive did not contain any evidence of the PhotoShow trash function being used.

A user can delete the digital photographs by using Windows Explorer and without using PhotoShow. When PhotoShow is started, it checks the existing albums and compares it to the digital photographs stored in the My Pictures subfolder. If the My Pictures subfolder has been deleted, PhotoShow will not display the album anymore even though the PhotoShow album information still exists.

An example of the user deleting an entire subfolder of photographs from the My Pictures folder was a subfolder named "Little 1." This subfolder was deleted on October 18, 2005 and was associated with a PhotoShow album that was created on October 15, 2005. The subfolder contained 41 digital photographs taken with a Minolta DiMAGE S414 camera. One of the original photographs, PICT0011.jpg, was deleted

by the user on October 16, 2005 (prior to the entire subfolder being deleted). All of these photos were located in the user's Recycle Bin folder. However, the PhotoShow album information associated with the "Little 1" album was still intact.

I also found a series of five digital photographs in the Windows Recycle Bin. Some of these photographs depicted the defendant posing nude with minors. These photographs were named as follows:

PICT0013.jpg

PICT0014.jpg

PICT0015.jpg

PICT0016.jpg

PICT0017.jpg

These photographs were taken with a Minolta DiMAGE S414 camera within a 30 second time period. The EXIF date on the photos was May 7, 2005 starting at 18:41 p.m. These photos were part of the [*redacted*] PhotoShow album, which was created on November 9, 2005 at 8:37 a.m. These photos were deleted by the user on November 9, 2005 and were originally located in a folder named [*redacted*], which was located in the user's My Pictures subfolder (C:\Documents and Settings\Karl\My Documents\My Pictures\[*redacted*]).

Registered Software

I checked the defendant's hard drive for registered software and located the following registration information:

Windows XP Pro

Name: Karl Jones

Organization: DNC

Microsoft Word 2002

Name: Karl Jones

Organization: DNC

Norton Systemworks 2005

Email: [*redacted*]@hotmail.com

Forte Agent Newsreader

Licensed to: Karl Jones

Detailed Analysis of Rewritable Optical Disc

When I first examined CD1, I found that CD1 had been formatted with Universal Disk Format (UDF), which is an industry standard file system for this type of optical disc. This specification allows data to be written to disc like a normal drive and data can be deleted.

If a user wants to copy and delete files on this type of optical disc, packet writing software needs to be installed on the computer. The defendant's computer had Nero's InCD software installed to handle this function.

Using InCD, a user can copy files directly to the CD-RW disc, similar to copying files to another hard drive or a floppy disk. A user can also delete specific files on the optical disc. In this scenario, deleting a file from a CD-RW disc does not permanently delete the file. The deleted file is still present as the UDF file system was simply modified to appear as though the file no longer exists. This deleted file is then considered to exist in the "unallocated space" of the disc.

A user can also erase a CD-RW disc. There are two options available to erasing a disc, full erase and quick erase. A full erase will completely delete all previous data and make the disc blank. A quick erase only erases the UDF file system structure so the disc appears blank; however, all previously existing data is still present and recoverable. This previously existing data would be considered to exist in the unallocated space of the disc.

I found 107 digital photographs that were visible in the allocated space of CD1. These photographs were located in the root folder and 3 subfolders:

4 girls

home102805

SAM & New girl

During my analysis of CD1, I noticed that there was 552,035,340 bytes of unallocated space. I examined the unallocated space and recovered 211 digital photographs (JPEG EXIF format).

Since these were recovered files which had been previously deleted, there were not any file names associated with these photographs. All of the photographs had been taken with a digital camera identified as:

Make: Minolta Co., Ltd.

Model: DiMAGE S414

Exhibit D lists all of the recovered digital photographs by item number and the date and time that each photograph was taken. It should be noted that this date and time is only as accurate as set by the user. If the user had incorrectly set the internal clock of the camera, then all photographs taken will reflect an inaccurate date and time.

Exhibits

This report contains the following exhibits:

Exhibit A PhotoShow Express interface and prompts

Exhibit B PhotoShow Album information

Exhibit C PhotoShow Express interface and prompts (Controlled Environment)

Exhibit D Recovered digital photograph information

EXHIBIT A

EXHIBIT A

You have selected photos from
Removable Disk (F:)

Would you like to erase ALL photos contained
on Removable Disk (F:) after your album is made?

EXHIBIT B

EXHIBIT C

EXHIBIT C

EXHIBIT D

Recovered Digital Photograph Information

Item #	Date/Time	Item #	Date/Time	Item #	Date/Time
1	2005:06:03 15:33:26	41	2005:05:07 18:39:44	81	2005:04:27 12:43:38
2	2005:06:03 15:33:29	42	2005:05:07 18:39:52	82	2005:04:27 12:43:46
3	2005:06:03 15:33:33	43	2005:05:07 18:40:26	83	2005:04:27 12:44:00
4	2005:06:03 15:33:46	44	2005:05:07 18:40:31	84	2005:04:27 12:44:08
5	2005:06:03 15:33:55	45	2005:05:07 18:40:37	85	2005:04:27 12:44:27
6	2005:06:03 15:34:01	46	2005:05:07 18:48:39	86	2005:04:27 12:44:40
7	2005:06:03 15:34:03	47	2005:05:07 18:48:43	87	2005:04:27 12:44:59
8	2005:06:03 15:34:31	48	2005:05:07 18:48:49	88	2005:04:27 12:45:04
9	2005:06:03 15:34:34	49	2005:05:07 18:48:52	89	2005:04:27 12:45:11
10	2005:06:03 15:34:43	50	2005:05:07 18:49:05	90	2005:04:27 12:48:56
11	2005:06:03 15:34:47	51	2005:05:07 18:49:09	91	2005:04:27 12:49:05
12	2005:07:13 21:09:20	52	2005:04:27 12:26:22	92	2005:04:27 12:49:10
122	2005:04:27 12:58:23	162	2005:04:26 21:37:22	202	2005:02:02 13:50:31
123	2005:04:27 12:58:31	163	2005:04:26 21:37:26	203	2005:02:02 13:50:34
124	2005:04:27 12:58:39	164	2005:04:26 21:37:51	204	2005:02:02 13:50:48
125	2005:04:27 12:59:38	165	2005:04:26 21:37:55	205	2005:02:02 13:54:43
126	2005:04:27 13:01:59	166	2005:04:26 21:37:58	206	2005:02:02 13:56:30
127	2005:04:27 13:02:06	167	2005:04:26 21:38:11	207	2005:02:02 13:56:39
128	2005:04:27 13:02:09	168	2005:04:26 21:38:18	208	2005:02:02 13:56:46
129	2005:04:27 13:02:13	169	2005:04:26 21:38:36	209	2005:02:02 13:57:12
130	2005:04:27 13:22:22	170	2005:04:26 21:38:40	210	2005:02:02 13:57:32
131	2005:04:27 13:22:29	171	2005:04:26 21:38:44	211	2005:02:02 13:57:39

Report #3

Summary

The defendant's computer was used to remotely connect to another computer in the residence, which belonged to his 10-year-old daughter. The defendant's computer used screen recording software to capture the activity being displayed on that computer. During those recording sessions, the defendant's 10 year old daughter was alone in her bedroom and intentionally using a live webcam connected to her computer. The webcam captured her nude while she was engaging in lascivious exhibition of her genitalia and simulated sexually explicit conduct. In addition to this activity being recorded by the defendant's computer, the webcam feed was broadcasted live on the Internet using a program called Camfrog.

List of Evidence Reviewed and Methodology

I conducted analysis of the following evidence:

1) Encase forensic images of a single hard drive that was installed in a computer located in the defendant's home. This image is identified as PC1, which came from an EMachine computer, model T3524, serial number ABC6AC0008865.

2) EnCase forensic image of a single hard drive that was installed in a computer located in the defendant's home. This image is identified as PC2, which came from an EMachine computer, model T3612, serial number ABC7310011745.

I verified the forensic images and zero errors were reported.

I examined the forensic image of the hard drive using EnCase Forensic Edition, which is a commercially available program.

Detailed Analysis

Operating System

When the defendant's computer (PC1) starts, the Windows operating system (XP Home Edition) is launched. There are two primary accounts (user profiles) that someone could use to login: Owner and Guest.

The Owner account is password protected and is the account that is actively used. The Guest account is not password protected and has not been used since October 16, 2007.

There is also a local administrator account that was last accessed on February 1, 2007.

Remote Desktop Control

I found a software program installed on the defendant's computer called Remote Desktop Control. This software was registered to Robert Jones, RJ Trucking Inc.

This software is designed to give the user administrative control over another computer that is running the remote agent software. For example, the administrator can view the desktop of another computer (View Only mode) or take over complete control (Full Control mode) as if the administrator was sitting in front of the remote computer using the keyboard.

This software was configured to connect to a remote computer with the computer name of AB3612. See Exhibit A for a screenshot of the actual user interface.

I have examined the forensic image of a hard drive from another computer seized from the defendant's residence, which was identified as evidence item PC2. The computer name of that operating system is AB3612.

Screen Recorder

I found a software program installed on the defendant's computer called Bluent's Screen Recorder v1.5. This software is designed to create a digital video of an entire desktop, a specific window, a region, or a HandiCam. See Exhibit B for a screenshot of the actual user interface.

When the user clicks the button to start recording, all of the video that is captured during that session is stored in a temporary file called srectmp1.avi, which is stored in the following folder: C:\Program Files\Screen Recorder\Temp

The user also has the ability to save the captured video in AVI (audio video interleave) format. By default, it will direct the user to store the video in the C:\Program Files\Screen Recorder folder; however, the user has the option to store the video in any folder.

During my examination, I found the following AVI video files associated with this screen capture program:

1. C:\Program Files\Screen Recorder\Temp\srectmp1.avi

2. C:\Program Files\Screen Recorder\A101607.avi

3. C:\Program Files\Screen Recorder\AB101607.avi

4. C:\Program Files\Screen Recorder\camgirl0929.avi

5. C:\Documents and Settings\Owner\Desktop\Temp\ Downloads\Pics\ 081707scrnrcd.avi

6. C:\Documents and Settings\Owner\Desktop\Temp\ Downloads\Pics\ ScrnRcrd\091907.avi

Information on these video files is located on Exhibit C.

The current screen recorder temp file (srectmp1.avi) was started on 10/16/07 at 4:12 PM at ran for 10 minutes and 19 seconds. That video was saved by the user as A101607.avi and contains the same video as srectmp1.avi except the last 56 seconds was excluded. The video was then saved by the user a second time as AB101607.avi, but only contains the first 1 minute and 48 seconds.

This screen recorder capture (srectmp1.avi) consisted of the user's entire desktop (defendant's computer PC1). The user had used the Remote Desktop Control software in View Only mode to view the remote computer desktop identified as AB3612.

The screen recorder capture of two parts: 1) The desktop of AB3612; and, 2) The defendant's Windows task bar, which is the bottom bar that consists of the Start button, task bar, and system tray. See Exhibit D for a screenshot of the recording named srectmp1.avi.

In the screenshot depicted in Exhibit C, the user on computer AB3612 is using a video chat software program called Camfrog. Camfrog allows the user to chat with other users on the Internet who are also using Camfrog. In this case, the user is logged into a video chat room called Camfrog_Adult_Lounge with a screenname of "Just_Fun_Chat."

Camfrog is displaying the user's video camera (webcam) in real time in a window titled "Your Video." This realtime capture is available for anyone else in the chat room to view. The user also has the ability to open up realtime video being shared by other users.

Since I have also reviewed the forensic image of evidence item PC2, I recognized the Windows Desktop being displayed in the Remote Desktop Control window. It belongs

to the [*redacted*] account on that computer, which belongs to the defendant's 10 year old daughter.

The defendant's 10 year old daughter was captured during each of the remote desktop recordings. The Camfrog webcam window displayed a live feed of her nude, engaged in lascivious exhibition of her genitalia and simulated sexually explicit conduct before a live webcam feed.

In the video recording dated October 16, 2007, it captured the user on the defendant's computer accessing Internet trucking websites and MapQuest directions on his computer, revealing that he watched the webcam feed from his desktop computer, but only paid attention when the daughter was onscreen engaging in sex acts.

Exhibits

This report also contains the following exhibit:

Exhibit A: User interface screenshot of Remote Desktop Control software

Exhibit B: User interface screenshot of Bluent's Screen Recorder software

Exhibit C: Screen Recorder video information

Exhibit D: Screenshot of the recording named srectmp1.avi

EXHIBIT A

EXHIBIT B

EXHIBIT C

Screen Recorder Videos

Name	File Created	Last Written	File Size (bytes)	Video Start Time	Video End Time	Length (h:mm:ss)
081707scrnrcd.avi	8/17/07 4:59 PM	8/17/07 5:01 PM	451,071,488	8/17/07 4:53 PM	8/17/07 4:56 PM	0:03:43
091907.avi	9/19/07 5:29 PM	9/19/07 5:29 PM	240,718,848	9/19/07 5:17 PM	9/19/07 5:18 PM	0:01:53
camgirl0929.avi	9/29/07 9:24 AM	9/29/07 9:24 AM	136,745,472	9/29/07 9:18 AM	9/29/07 9:19 AM	0:00:51
srectmp1.avi	8/17/07 4:42 PM	10/16/07 4:22 PM	1,277,363,200	10/16/07 4:12 PM	10/16/07 4:22 PM	0:10:19
101607.avi	10/16/07 4:23 PM	10/16/07 4:25 PM	1,169,001,472	10/16/07 4:12 PM	10/16/07 4:22 PM	0:09:23
101607.avi	10/16/07 4:27 PM	10/16/07 4:27 PM	228,884,480	10/16/07 4:12 PM	10/16/07 4:14 PM	0:01:48

EXHIBIT D

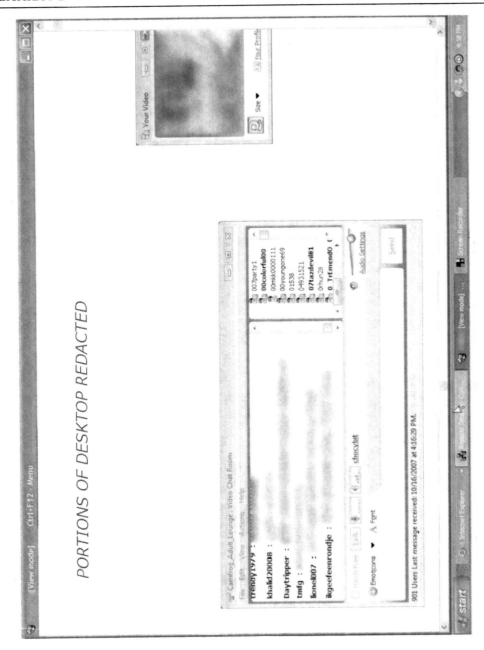

PORTIONS OF DESKTOP REDACTED

Report #4

Summary

I conducted a preliminary examination of the five electronic items brought to our office by Detective Jones. A search warrant authorized the search of these devices for evidence of child exploitation.

One of the cell phones (Item #3: LG Optimus) and attached memory card contained digital videos and images depicting child pornography.

The generic-brand tower computer (Item #5) contained digital videos and images depicting child pornography. This computer was used to send and receive files depicting child pornography to other computer users across the Internet using a chat program called Skype.

List of Items Reviewed and Methodology

Prior to conducting my examination, I reviewed the reports and search warrant authorizing the search of the electronic devices for evidence of child exploitation.

I checked the items out from the evidence custodian. There were three cellular telephones and two tower computers, which are listed below as Items 1 through 5.

Item#1: Cell Phone, Nokia, N97-3, no serial number

This device contained the following items:

1) SanDisk Micro SD memory card

2) T-Mobile SIM card, S/N: 9999-60361-45677-1234

I attempted to power up the phone, by depressing the power button, but the phone would not turn on. I could not use any software to examine the phone as it would not power up.

I removed the SIM card and used a Cellebrite UFED device to extract any information from the SIM card. The SIM card contained the following information:

ICCID: 9999603614567771234

IMSI: 805260365677530

I removed the Micro SD card from the phone and attached it to my lab computer running Windows 7 Professional using a write-protected Addonics memory card reader. The write-protection permits data to be copied from the memory card, while preventing any data being written to it. Using AccessData's FTK Imager, I created an Encase image of the Micro SD memory card. Upon completion, I verified the image and placed the memory card back into the phone.

Item#2: Cell Phone, LG, Optimus M (MS690), CDMA, S/N: 104KPYR0673882

This device contained a SanDisk Micro SD memory card

I started my examination of this cell phone by first powering up the phone and placing it into "airplane mode". Airplane mode allows the user to use many of the phones features, such as games, notepad, and voice memos when the user is onboard an airplane or in any other area where making or receiving calls or data is prohibited. When the phone is in airplane mode, it cannot send or receive any calls or access any on-line information.

I connected the device to my lab computer and used DataPilot's SecureView 3 software to extract the phone data.

I removed the Micro SD card from the phone and attached it to my lab computer running Windows 7 Professional using a write-protected Addonics memory card reader. Using AccessData's FTK Imager, I created an Encase image of the Micro SD memory card. Upon completion, I verified the image and placed the memory card back into the phone.

Item#3: Cell Phone, Apple, iPhone 3G, (A1241), White, S/N: 99929FJY1R4

I removed the SIM card and used a Cellebrite UFED device to extract information from the SIM card.

The SIM card contained the following information:

ICCID: 99994104212238561234

IMSI: 805613006199456

I replaced the SIM card back into the iPhone and powered it up. I immediately placed it into airplane mode, which turns off the phone transceiver. I connected the iPhone to

my lab computer and used DataPilot's SecureView 3 software to extract the phone data.

Item#4: Computer, Compaq, Presario 8000, tower enclosure, S/N: 00043-422-520-222

I conducted an exterior and interior examination of this computer and found it contained the following two hard drives:

1) Maxtor, DiamondMax 21, IDE, 320GB, S/N: 5QF1TK26

2) Seagate, ST380020A, IDE, 80GB, S/N:5GCMDKZ1 (not connected)

I disconnected and removed the 320 GB Maxtor hard drive from the desktop computer. I connected the Maxtor hard drive to my lab computer using a Tableau write-protect device. This device permits data to be copied from a hard drive, while preventing any data being written to it.

I started my forensic computer with Windows 7 Professional and made an Encase forensic image of the Maxtor hard drive using AccessData's FTK Imager software. Upon completion, I verified the image and placed the hard drive back into the desktop computer.

I removed the Seagate hard drive from the desktop computer. It was not connected to any cables within the computer. I connected it to my lab computer using the same Tableau write-protect device. The hard drive did not spin up. I was unable to create an image or analyze any data from the Seagate drive as it was not functioning at all.

I used Encase Forensic Edition (version 6.19.4) to conduct my analysis of the forensic image of the Maxtor hard drive.

Item#5: Computer, Generic brand, black, tower enclosure, no serial number

I conducted an exterior and interior examination of this computer and found it contained the following hard drive: Maxtor, DiamondMax Plus 9, IDE, 120GB, S/N: Y340NPDE

I disconnected and removed the 120 GB Maxtor hard drive from the desktop computer. I connected the Maxtor hard drive to my lab computer using a Tableau write-protect device.

I started my forensic computer with Windows 7 Professional and made an Encase forensic image of the Maxtor hard drive using AccessData's FTK Imager software. Upon completion, I verified the image and placed the hard drive back into the desktop computer.

I used Encase Forensic Edition (version 6.19.4) to conduct my analysis of the forensic image of the Maxtor hard drive.

I used Paraben's Chat Examiner software to analyze the user's Skype data.

Detailed Analysis

Item#1: Cellular Phone, Nokia, N97-3

The memory card contained several folders, such as "Videos", "DCIM", and "Music" folders. These folders commonly store files created or downloaded by the user of the phone.

The "Videos" folder contained several video files, but none that contained any children performing any elicit acts.

The "DCIM" folder was empty, except for some thumbnail graphics that appeared to be from the user's web cache.

The "Music" folder contained several "MP3" music files, with Spanish names.

There was no evidence of child exploitation found on the memory card.

Item#2: Cellular Phone, LG, Optimus M (MS690)

The phone contained the following types of information:

Phone number: (805) 396-1234

Service Provider: Metro PCS

55 "Contacts"

4211 Inbox "Messages" & 4142 Outbox "Messages"

Call History: Dialed-126, Received-68, Missed-25

Additional information is attached in the SecureView 3 report (LG phone).

The phone contained 347 digital photographs. Of those 47 images, the following 4 images depicted child pornography:

1) #247, which was named "j.jpg." This image depicts [*redacted*].

2) #265, which was named "big.jpg." This image depicts [*redacted*].

3) #297, which was named "clu pthc 2010 03 23 003897.jpg." This image depicts [*redacted*].

4) #298, which was named "kinderkutje ls model - [*redacted*].jpg." This image depicts [*redacted*].

The SanDisk SD memory card contained 25 digital movies in a folder called Videos. Of those 25 movies, the following 11 movies depicted child pornography:

1) pthc pedo rare [*redacted*].mp4

2) 6YO GOOD.mp4

3) Pthc 7yo girl [*redacted*].mp4

4) 2011 PTHC 6yo little blond [*redacted*].mp4

5) Pthc Pedoland Frifam 2010 9yo-[*redacted*].mp4

6) 2010 pthc [*redacted*].mp4

7) Pthc [*redacted*].mp4

8) pthc Pedoland Frifam 9yo [*redacted*].mp4

9) (Pthc) [*redacted*].mp4

10) Hussyfan - pthc - [*redacted*].mp4

11) kinder[*redacted*].mp4

Item#3: Cell Phone, Apple, iPhone 3G

The phone contained the following information:

Service Provider: AT & T

Contacts: 37

Messages: Inbox = 4370; Outbox = 4695

Call History: Dialed = 80; Received = 14; Missed = 6

The phone contained 97 digital photographs and no digital videos. None of the digital photographs depicted child pornography.

The phone did not contain evidence of child exploitation.

Additional information is attached in the SecureView 3 report (Apple iPhone).

Item#4: Computer, Compaq, Presario 8000

My initial analysis of the 320GB Maxtor hard drive revealed the following information:

> Operating system: Microsoft Windows XP (Installed 05/06/2008)

> Registered owner: "New User"

> Time Zone: Pacific Daylight Time (-7:00 GMT)

> BIOS date and time were accurate, compared to the current date and time

The operating system had two active user accounts: Administrator and Guest.

I conducted an examination of the following common folders of the operating system: My Documents, My Pictures, My Videos, and Desktop. I did not find any evidence of child exploitation.

I recovered several deleted files; however, none of the recovered files depicted any type of child exploitation.

Item#5: Computer, Generic brand, black

My initial analysis of the 320GB Maxtor hard drive revealed the following information:

> Operating system: Microsoft Windows XP (installed 05/19/2011)

> Registered owner: "Admin"

> Time Zone: Central Daylight Time (-5:00 GMT)

> BIOS date and time were accurate, compared to the current date and time

The operating system had two active user accounts: Administrator and Guest.

The Administrator account was password-protected. Using AccessData's Password Recovery ToolKit, I was able to decrypt the password for this account, which was "preteen."

I conducted an examination of the following common folders in the Administrator's user profile: My Documents, My Pictures, My Videos, and Desktop.

My Documents Folder

The user's My Documents folder contained the following four digital images that depicted child pornography:

1) "Clu pthc 2010 03 23 003897.jpg

2) kinderkutje ls model - [*redacted*].jpg

3) 131_pthc_ultra_hussyfan_9_y.jpg

4) (pthc [*redacted*].jpg

Items 1 and 2 were also found on the LG Optimus M cell phone.

The user's My Documents folder contained the following three digital videos that depicted child pornography:

1) (pthc) broder [*redacted*].mpg

2) pthc hussyfan 9yr.mpg

3) pthc new 2011 12yr [*redacted*].wmv

The user's My Documents folder contained a subfolder called "PTHC," which I know stands for "Pre-Teen Hard Core." This subfolder contained eight digital video files in 3GP format that depicted child pornography:

1) (Asian Lolita) [*redacted*].3gp

2) (Hussyfan) (pthc) [*redacted*].3gp

3) (Kinderkutje) (Pedo) Pedoland [*redacted*].3gp

4) (Kingpass) (Pthc) (Liluplanet) [*redacted*].3gp

5) (Kleuterkutje) (Frifam) (Ptsc) !!! NEW !!! [*redacted*].3gp

6) (Lolita-Sf-Model) Ls-Magazine - Issue [*redacted*].3gp

7) (lsm ls-magazine 08-07-02 (Complete) [*redacted*].3gp

8) (Asian Lolita) Kids [*redacted*].3gp

Note: 3GP is a common video format used on popular cellular phone models.

The user's My Documents folder contained subfolders named "Shareaza" and "Shareaza Downloads." The "Shareaza" folder was empty. However the "Shareaza

Downloads" folder contained 93 video files of various formats, all with file names relating to "PTHC" or child pornography (such as "11yo Dark Video," "Lolitas House," "Asian Lolita," etc.). Many of the videos showed females under the age of 10 years performing sex acts with adult males.

"Shareaza" is a commonly known peer-to-peer (P2P) file sharing program similar to Napster.

My Pictures Folder

The user's My Pictures folder contained 138 digital images. Two of these images were also found on the LG Optimus M cell phone:

1) big.jpg

2) j.jpg.

My Videos Folder

The user's My Videos folder contained numerous digital video files of various file types. However, the following 14 video files depicted child pornography:

1) Pedo (Pthc) - [redacted].3gp

2) zooskool- PTHC - [redacted].3gp

3) 6YO GOOD.3gp

4) Love_[redacted].3gp

5) pthc 2009 new [redacted].3gp

6) Pthc 2009 [redacted].3gp

7) Pthc - Pedofilia [redacted].3gp

8) Preview-T-48750620-[redacted].3gp

9) (Pthc) [redacted].3gp

10) Pthc - 7Yo 9Yo [redacted].3gp

11) pthc 2010 [redacted].3gp

12) PTHC - [redacted].3gp

13) rape [redacted].3gp

14) ohya.3gp

Desktop Folder

The user's Desktop contained four adult pornography videos. This folder also contained five digital images of an adult male who was taking pictures of himself in the mirror using his cellular phone.

Hash Analysis

I conducted hash analysis of the files stored on the hard drive specifically looking for files depicting child pornography. I used a hash set maintained by DHS-ICE (Department of Homeland Security – Immigration and Customs Enforcement) for use in child exploitation investigations.

In simple terms, hash analysis is the process of calculating a mathematical value for each file and then comparing those values against the hash set for possible matching values. A matching value would indicate a positive match for known child pornography.

This hash analysis resulted in a match of 27 digital videos located in the "Shareaza Downloads" folder. The two digital images found in the user's My Pictures folder also matched.

iPhone Backup Folder

The Administrator user profile contained 3 backup folders for Apple devices, such as iPod, iPhone, and iPad, that have been connected to the computer . These folders were located in the user's Application Data folder: Apple Computer\MobileSync\Backup. Two of the backup folders contained a file called "Info.plist". This file identifies which device the backup belongs to. Inside both "Info.plist" files contained information relating to the following information:

Display Name: MARCO'S IPHONE

IMEI: 805613006199456

Serial Number: 99929FJY1R4

NOTE: The IMEI and the serial numbers in the "Info.plist" files are the same as the iPhone listed above.

Several of the pictures found inside the backup folders were of the same male adult that was in the pictures found in the Administrator's Desktop folder.

Skype

There was a Skype account associated with the Administrator user profile. The Skype username (UserID) was "super[redacted]".

The UserID of super[redacted] listed a full name of "frisco" and an email address of "[redacted]@yahoo.com". This Skype account contains 83 other Skype UserIDs in the contact list. This Skype user both sent and received various pictures and video files to the following 3 Skype contacts:

1) [redacted]

2) [redacted]

3) [redacted]

The Chat Examiner report shows that after adding these 3 UserIDs to super[redacted]'s contact list, he immediately asks them, "hello want to trade pthc videos?"

The Chat Examiner report also shows which files were uploaded or downloaded, along with the location, on the computer, where it was stored. For example; the Chat log shows a file named, "(pthc pedo) [redacted].avi" was uploaded from "C:\Documents and Settings\Administrator\My Documents\Shareaza Downloads\" to the Skype UserID "[redacted]" on 07/25/2011 at 8:48 AM.

I found the same file named "(pthc pedo) [redacted].avi" in the "C:\Documents and Settings\Administrator\My Documents\Shareaza Downloads\" folder.

During the same chat session, there was a picture file named, "clu pthc 2010 03 23 003897.jpg" that was downloaded from the Skype UserID "[redacted]" on 07/25/2011 @ 8:55 AM to the folder, "C:\Documents and Settings\Administrator\My Documents\". I confirmed that this same file still existed in the user's My Documents folder.

I found several of the digital videos and image files listed in the "File Transfer History" section of the Chat Examiner Report on the suspect's hard drive.

There were a total of 63 digital videos and images that were transferred between the suspect's computer and the three Skype UserID's listed above during the time period between 06/07/2011 and 07/25/2011.

During a chat conversation with Skype UserID "[*redacted*]," which is one of the suspect's other Skype contacts, he admits that he knows "PTHC" is "child porn" and that it is illegal in the USA.

See Chat Examiner Report for additional information regarding the above mentioned chat sessions as well as the File Transfer History.

Personal Photographs

I noticed that several of the personal digital photographs stored either on the cell phones or on the attached SD memory cards, consisted of the same adult male. Some of these photos were also found in the Administrator's user profile, as well as the Apple iPhone backup folders.

Disposition

Electronic copies of this report, as well as reports from SecureView, CelleBrite, Chat Examiner, and EnCase were copied to a DVD for the Investigating Officer.

Appendix B:
VMware Virtual Host

This section will take you through an easy, step-by-step process to use a forensic image, such as an EnCase E01 evidence file or a dd image, as the virtual hard drive of a VMware virtual host. By booting the suspect's Windows-based computer using VMware Workstation, you can get a better perspective of how the suspect used the computer and take some screenshots that you can use in your report.

This section will not only walk you through the setup process, it will provide details so you can understand what is going in the background in case you need to troubleshoot this custom environment.

At this time, instructions are provided for the following Windows operating systems:

- Windows XP
- Windows Vista
- Windows 7

Getting Started

Start by installing the following software on a Windows 7 computer:

1) FTK Imager (version 3.1.4.6)
2) VMware Workstation (version 10.0.1)
3) VMware Virtual Disk Development Kit (version 5.1.1), which can be downloaded from www.vmware.com/support/developer/vddk
4) Freeware utility called Virtual Host QnP[§], which is a program created by the author specifically designed to help you "Query and Patch" the virtual environment.

To build the virtual environment, you will be following these 7 steps:

1) Mount the evidence
2) Query the registry hives of the mounted evidence
3) Build a VMware machine
4) Create a snapshot of the new machine
5) Patch the registry of the new machine and add drivers as necessary
6) Start the VMware machine
7) Install VMware Tools and other tweaks as desired

User Account Control (UAC): If you have UAC enabled on your computer, you will receive prompts to allow changes to be made. You will need to select Yes as escalated privileges are necessary to complete this process.

Step 1: Mounting Your Evidence

Connect the drive containing your forensic image, such as an EnCase E01 evidence file or a dd image, to your computer. You should use a drive with fast interface, such as eSATA or USB 3. Do not use USB 2 as it will be very slow for this type of process.

1) Start FTK Imager and select the Image Mounting icon on the toolbar

§ Request your copy by sending an email to info@pixleyforensics.com

2) Select the forensic image and the Mount Type should be set to Physical & Logical. Set the Drive Letter to Next Available and the Mount Method to Block Device / Read Only. Click the Mount button.

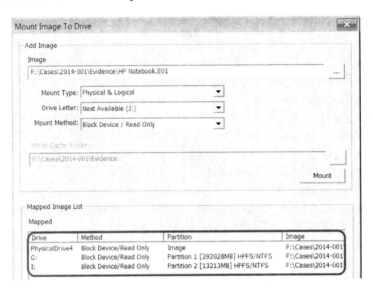

After the image is mounted, some of the key pieces of information that you will need to know during the setup of the VMware machine will be displayed in the Mapped Image List pane.

In this example, the image was mounted as Physical Drive 4 and the partition containing the operating system is mounted as logical drive G.

If you had already conducted some forensic analysis of this image, you will likely know which partition contains the operating system. However, if you are just getting started and are uncertain which is the correct partition, take a quick look at the mounted partitions using Windows Explorer. In this particular example. Windows Explorer showed that drive G: was identified as Local Disk (G:), and it clearly had the operating system. Drive I: had a volume label called RECOVERY.

Step 2: Query the Registry Hives

Before you start to build the VMware machine, you need to know some basic information about the installed operating system, including the architecture (32-bit or 64-bit) of the target computer.

Since the operating system of the target computer is mounted as a logical drive, you will be conducting your query through that mapped drive letter.

1. Launch Virtual Host QnP and click the Query Registry Hive button.

2. The will open a window that will prompt you to select the folder that contains the guest SYSTEM and SOFTWARE registry hives (\Windows\System32\config). Select the mounted logical drive containing the operating system, navigate to that folder, and click OK.

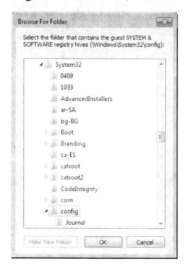

The main menu will display "Working…" as the program is querying the SYSTEM and SOFTWARE hives.

Behind the scenes, the program is querying for the following information:

1. Identify the Current Control Set (SYSTEM hive)

 Subkey: Select

 Value Name: Current

2. Identify the OS platform architecture (SYSTEM hive)

 Subkey: Controlset*nnn*\Control\Session Manager\Environment

 Value Name: PROCESSOR_ARCHITECTURE

3. Identify the last shutdown time (SYSTEM hive)

 Subkey: ControlSet*nnn*\Control\Windows

 Value Name: ShutdownTime

4. Identify the time zone information (SYSTEM hive)

 Subkey: ControlSet*nnn*\Control\TimeZoneInformation

 Value Name: ActiveTimeBias

5. Identify the installed OS (SOFTWARE hive)

 Subkey: Microsoft\Windows NT\CurrentVersion

 Value Name: ProductName

Once the query is complete, a Notice window will open and display the information you will need to build the VMware machine.

Leave this window open as you continue to the next step as you will refer back to this information.

Step 3: Build a VMware Machine

1. Start VMware Workstation 10. If VMware was already running prior to you mounting the evidence file with FTK Imager, close VMware and restart it. Select Create a New Virtual Machine.

2. Select Custom.

3. Select Workstation 10.0 for Hardware compatibility

4. Select "I will install the operating system later"

5. Select the guest operating system based on the information you gathered during the query above, which is displayed in the Notice window.

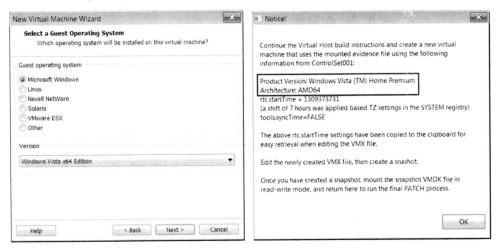

6. Set the name of the new virtual machine and the location of where the virtual machine files will be stored.

 Ideally, this data should be stored on a separate drive (not on the same drive as your OS or the evidence files) and in an empty folder. You want to ensure that data can be accessed as fast as possible, so use a drive with an eSATA or USB 3 interface.

7. Set the processor configuration. You may accept the default settings.

8. Set the amount of memory based on the recommendation. You can always increase the amount of memory later if necessary.

9. **IMPORTANT:** Set the Network Type to "**Do not use a network connection**." You do not want the target computer connecting to the Internet. Since you will be running the target computer in a live state, it will attempt to connect to the Internet or attack other computers if infected with malware.

10. Select the appropriate I/O SCSI controller type based on the recommendation. The recommendation will be based on the selected operating system:

Windows XP:	BusLogic
Windows Vista:	LSI Logic
Windows 7:	LSI Logic SAS

11. For all operating systems, select SCSI as the Disk Type.

12. Select physical disk.

13. Set the Device Physical Drive number based on FTK Imager and select Use entire disk.

14. Set the Disk File name to "Mounted Image.vmdk" (be sure to include the file extension).

15. The new virtual machine wizard is complete. Click Finish.

16. Close VMware as you need to make some edits to the configuration file.

Step 4: Create a Snapshot

1. Using Windows Explorer, go to the folder containing the new VMware machine.

At this time, the folder contains the following files:

1) [*machine name*].vmx Virtual machine configuration file
2) Mounted Image.vmdk VMware virtual disk file
3) [*machine name*].vmxf Supplemental configuration file
4) [*machine name*].vmsd Snapshot metadata

2. Use a text editor and open the .vmx file so you can make some edits.

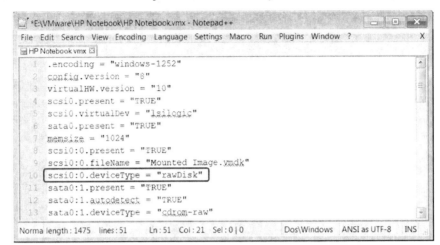

Within this file, you will see the following lines:

scsi0:0.fileName = "Mounted Image.vmdk"
scsi0:0.deviceType = "rawDisk"

Edit the deviceType line by changing "rawDisk" to "Disk"

Note: If you do not make this simple change to "Disk" then VMware will not allow you to create a snapshot.

3. Keep the .vmx file open so you can set the VMware Real Time Clock (RTC)

VMware has a function that allows you to set the date and time of the virtual machine BIOS. This allows you to backdate the machine to the time it was last running.

In order to set the time, you need to know the last shutdown time, which is stored in the registry in UTC time. This information was extracted from the registry during the query process. Along with the shutdown time, the time zone information was also extracted.

VMware needs this information written in UNIX time format, which has been automatically converted for you (including the correct time zone offset).

This information is displayed in the Notice window.

This time information was copied to the clipboard for you so you can quickly paste it into the .vmx file. Scroll to the bottom of the file and put the cursor on the last line. Press Ctrl+V to paste the information.

4. Save the changes to the .vmx file and close the text editor.

Note: If you ever look at this file in the future, you will see that VMware will reorganize the order of the line items so do not expect to see your added entries at the bottom of this file.

Important: Future Reference

Take a peek at Mounted Image.vmdk using a text editor. This file is called a disk *descriptor* file. Within this file, you will see a line similar to:

RW 312500000 FLAT "\\.\PhysicalDrive4" 0

This line describes the physical disk, which in this case is really a forensic image. RW is the access type (read write) and the following number is the total number of sectors. FLAT means all of the disk space has been allocated and the trailing 0 is the disk offset.

If you ever mount the forensic image in the future and the Physical Drive number changes, you will need to make a simple edit of this line to reflect the new drive number, such as:

RW 312500000 FLAT "\\.\PhysicalDrive6" 0

5. Double-click on the .vmx file to open the new machine in VMware.

6. As you go forward, you will need a place to store your changes to the VMware machine. Since your evidence file is read-only, you need to create a snapshot and all changes that occur while the machine is running will be written into the snapshot files. Select VM, Take Snapshot.

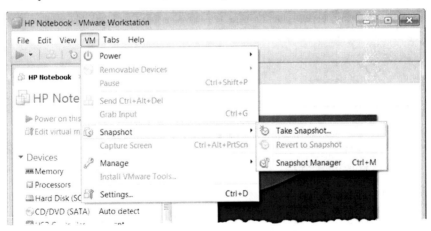

7. Set the snapshot name to Baseline.

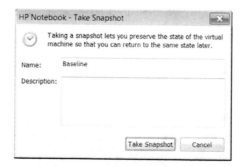

The snapshot process is very quick. Once it is completed, you will see the snapshot information displayed in the Virtual Machine Details section.

8. Close VMware.

If you look at the VMware machine folder, you will see all of the new snapshot files that have been created.

The file called Mounted Image-000001.vmdk is the primary descriptor file of the new snapshot and the one that you will be mounting in Step 5.

As a side note, the .vmx file has been updated to reflect the snapshot. The line with the scsi0:0.fileName now displays:

scsi0:0.fileName = "Mounted Image-000001.vmdk"

Step 5: Patch the Registry

You now need to make a couple of edits within the snapshot. When the original hard drive was inside the suspect's computer, the operating system was configured to boot based on hardware inside that computer. You have now technically transplanted that hard drive into a virtual environment, so you will need to make some simple edits so it will boot properly.

The first thing you need to do is mount the snapshot using a command line tool called vmware-mount.exe, which is part of the VMware Virtual Disk Development Kit (VDDK).

1. Start off by using the tool to display the partitions just to make sure your syntax is correct and ensure that your new snapshot can be read properly. Open a command prompt as Administrator and change directory to the following directory:

 "C:\Program Files (x86)\VMware\VMware Virtual Disk Development Kit\bin"

 Type the following syntax and make sure you select the snapshot vmdk file:

 vmware-mount.exe /p "[*path*]\Mounted Image-000001.vmdk"

```
Administrator: Command Prompt                                    _  □  x

Microsoft Windows [Version 6.1.7601]
Copyright (c) 2009 Microsoft Corporation.  All rights reserved.

C:\Windows\system32>cd "\Program Files (x86)\VMware\VMware Virt
ual Disk Development Kit\bin"

C:\Program Files (x86)\VMware\VMware Virtual Disk Development K
it\bin>vmware-mount.exe /p "e:\VMware\HP Notebook\Mounted Image
-000001.vmdk"
Volume  1 :   292028 MB, HPFS/NTFS
Volume  2 :    13213 MB, HPFS/NTFS

C:\Program Files (x86)\VMware\VMware Virtual Disk Development K
it\bin>
```

This will match what you saw in FTK Imager when you mounted the forensic image earlier. Make note of the volume number that contains the operating system (in this example, it is volume 1).

2. Mount the VMware snapshot in write-mode.

 You will now use the same tool to mount the snapshot in read/write mode as a new logical drive. The proper syntax is:

 vmware-mount.exe /v:1 /m:w N: "[*path*]\Mounted Image-000001.vmdk"

 Instead of typing this syntax out, just use the up arrow key within the command prompt to display your last command. Then use the left arrow key to move the cursor back and replace the /p with the new switches: /v:1 /m:w N:

 Press Enter when you have it correct.

 Based on the example syntax, this will mount the snapshot .vmdk in write mode (/m:w) using the first volume (/v:1) as logical drive letter N: on your computer (or select any other available drive letter).

```
Administrator: Command Prompt                                    _  □  ✕

Microsoft Windows [Version 6.1.7601]
Copyright (c) 2009 Microsoft Corporation.  All rights reserved.

C:\Windows\system32>cd "\Program Files (x86)\VMware\VMware Virt
ual Disk Development Kit\bin"

C:\Program Files (x86)\VMware\VMware Virtual Disk Development K
it\bin>vmware-mount.exe /p "e:\VMware\HP Notebook\Mounted Image
-000001.vmdk"
Volume  1 :   292028 MB, HPFS/NTFS
Volume  2 :    13213 MB, HPFS/NTFS

C:\Program Files (x86)\VMware\VMware Virtual Disk Development K
it\bin>vmware-mount.exe /v:1 /m:w N: "e:\VMware\HP Notebook\Mou
nted Image-000001.vmdk"

C:\Program Files (x86)\VMware\VMware Virtual Disk Development K
it\bin>_
```

To give you some perspective of this entire process, starting with the forensic image, you have now mounted and chained a few layers of read-only data to get to the point that you can write data.

3. It is now time to patch the snapshot using Virtual Host QnP. Close the Notice window by clicking OK. Click the Patch Virtual Host button.

Select the \Windows\System32 folder in the drive of the mounted snapshot (drive N:) and click OK.

The Virtual Host QnP program will patch the registry of the target computer. The patch that is applied will depend on the installed operating system:

Windows XP Professional

The SYSTEM hive is modified and files are updated:

1) Add the VMware SCSI driver as a service and start it during the boot process.
2) Add Critical Device Database services associated with the VMware SCSI driver and isapnp.
3) Copy the VMware SCSI driver (vmscsi.sys) to the \Windows\system32\drivers folder
4) Patch winlogon.exe.

Windows Vista

The SYSTEM hive is modified:

1) Start the LSI Logic driver as a service during the boot process.
2) Modify the Windows Crash Control to not Auto Reboot upon failure.

Windows 7

The SYSTEM hive is modified:

1) Start the LSI Logic SAS driver as a service during the boot process.
2) Modify the Windows Crash Control to not Auto Reboot upon failure.

After the snapshot is properly patched, Virtual Host QnP will display a window indicating the process is finished. Click OK and the program will close.

4. Unmount the VMware snapshot.

 Now that the changes have been made, you will need to unmount the snapshot. The proper syntax to unmount the snapshot is:

 vmware-mount.exe /d [*drive_letter*]

 The /d switch means delete the mapping to the virtual drive letter. In this example, the syntax would be:

 vmware-mount.exe /d N:

 If you get an error that the drive could not be unmounted, which is common, try the syntax again and add the /f (force) switch:

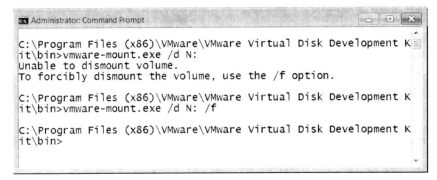

Step 6: Start The New VMware Machine

Start VMware as Administrator and then click Power on this virtual machine.

If you fail to start VMware as Administrator, you may receive the follow error message (Insufficient permission to access file). This type of error message is associated with your UAC settings.

Depending on how Windows was shutdown down prior to imaging the hard drive, you may receive an error message during the boot process. For example, a computer that was in hibernation mode will display the following type of error:

> Windows Boot Manager
>
> Your computer can't come out of hibernation.
>
> Status: 0x0000411
>
> Info: A fatal error occurred processing the restoration data.
>
> File: \hiberfil.sys
>
> Any information that was not saved before the computer went into hibernation will be lost.

After pressing the Enter key, the system will restart and the normal login screen will appear.

Password-Protected Login Account

When Windows starts up, you may discover that the local user account requires a password to login. Prior to attempting to defeat the password, you may want to take a screenshot of the login window if you want to use it in the future as a demonstrative exhibit. VMware has a built-in screen capture tool, which can be activated by selecting Ctrl+Alt+PrtScn or use the pulldown menu (VM, Capture Screen). A screenshot file in .png format will be saved to your Desktop.

If the machine has a password, you can use a tool like Ophcrack to break the password using pre-calculated tables or forcibly clear the password by editing the registry. The following method will walk you through clearing the password with Offline Windows Password & Registry Editor Boot CD[**]. You will need to download the ISO image, which is very small (about 17 MB).

1. With the virtual machine powered off, click on the CD/DVD drive to open the Virtual Machine Settings.

2. Select CD/DVD, Use ISO image file, and select the ISO image.

[**] The boot CD is a free download from http://pogostick.net/~pnh/ntpasswd/

3. Boot the VMware machine by selecting VM, Power, Power On to BIOS

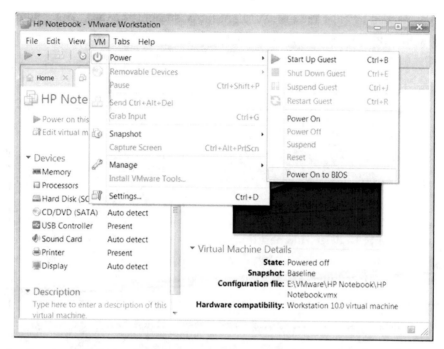

4. Set the BIOS boot order with the CD-ROM drive as the first boot device.

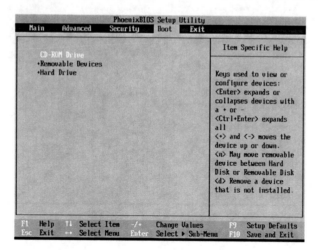

5. Exit the BIOS using Exit Saving Changes. The machine will immediately reboot using the boot CD.

Boot CD Walkthrough

The steps needed to clear the password are fairly straight forward. This section will walk you through the basic steps of using this Linux boot CD and if you need further guidance, refer to the FAQ page on the boot CD creator's website.

1) At the boot prompt, click Enter.

```
Press enter to boot, or give linux kernel boot options first if needed.
Some that I have to use once in a while:
boot nousb          - to turn off USB if not used and it causes problems
boot irqpoll        - if some drivers hang with irq problem messages
boot nodrivers      - skip automatic disk driver loading

boot:
```

2) It will attempt to detect the partition containing the Windows installation. If the partition number is correct, press Enter. Otherwise, type the correct partition number and press Enter.

```
==================================================================
¤ Step ONE: Select disk where the Windows installation is
==================================================================
n device bytes      GB  MB  === DISK PARTITIONS:
1 sda1    299036672  285 292028
2 sda2    13530112   12  13212

292028 MB partition sda1 is NTFS. Found windows on: Windows/System32/config
13213 MB partition sda2 is NTFS. No windows there
==================================================================
--- Possible windows installation found:
 1 sda1          292028 MB Windows/System32/config

Please select partition by number or
 q = quit
 d = automatically start disk drivers
 m = manually select disk drivers to load
 f = fetch additional drivers from floppy / usb
 a = show all partitions found (fdisk)
 l = show propbable Windows partitions only
Select: [1]
```

3) To clear the password, you will want to select the SAM hive. Since 1 is the default setting, press Enter.

```
============================================================
¤ Step TWO: Select registry files
============================================================

-rwxrwxrwx    2 0          0         262144 Jun  9  2008 BCD-Template
-rwxrwxrwx    2 0          0        6815744 Jun 29  2011 COMPONENTS
-rwxrwxrwx    1 0          0         262144 Jun 29  2011 DEFAULT
drwxrwxrwx    1 0          0              0 Nov  2  2006 Journal
drwxrwxrwx    1 0          0           8192 Jul  8  2011 RegBack
-rwxrwxrwx    1 0          0         262144 Jun 29  2011 SAM
-rwxrwxrwx    1 0          0         262144 Jun 29  2011 SECURITY
-rwxrwxrwx    1 0          0       15728640 Jun 29  2011 SOFTWARE
-rwxrwxrwx    1 0          0        9175040 Jun 29  2011 SYSTEM
drwxrwxrwx    1 0          0           4096 Jun  9  2008 TxR
drwxrwxrwx    1 0          0           4096 Mar 31 10:02 systemprofile

Select which part of registry to load, use predefined choices
or list the files with space as delimiter
1 - Password reset [sam]
2 - RecoveryConsole parameters [software]
3 - Load almost all of it for regedit tec [system software sam security]
q - quit - return to previous
[1] :
```

4) You will want to edit the user data and passwords. Since 1 is the default option, press Enter.

```
============================================================
¤ Step THREE: Password or registry edit
============================================================
chntpw version 1.00 140201, (c) Petter N Hagen
Hive <SAM> name (from header): <\SystemRoot\System32\Config\SAM>
ROOT KEY at offset: 0x001020 * Subkey indexing type is: 666c <lf>
File size 262144 [40000] bytes, containing 7 pages (+ 1 headerpage)
Used for data: 321/57632 blocks/bytes, unused: 4/3584 blocks/bytes.

<>========<> chntpw Main Interactive Menu <>========<>
Loaded hives: <SAM>
  1 - Edit user data and passwords
  2 - Syskey status & change
  3 - RecoveryConsole settings
    - - -
  9 - Registry editor, now with full write support!
  q - Quit (you will be asked if there is something to save)

  What to do? [1] ->
```

5) You need to select the user account that you want to clear the password. If the account relative identifier (RID) is selected as default (within brackets at the prompt), then press Enter. Otherwise, enter the RID of the account that you want to select.

```
===== chntpw Edit User Info & Passwords ====

| RID -|---------- Username -----------| Admin? |- Lock? --|
| 01f4 | Administrator               | ADMIN  | dis/lock |
| 01f5 | Guest                       |        | dis/lock |
| 03ea | mikey                       | ADMIN  |          |

Please enter user number (RID) or 0 to exit: [3e8]
```

6) At the User Edit menu, press 1 and Enter to clear the user password.

```
================= USER EDIT =================
RID      : 1000 [03e8]
Username: mikey
fullname:
comment :
homedir :

00000220 = Administrators (which has 2 members)

Account bits: 0x0214 =
[ ] Disabled       | [ ] Homedir req.   | [X] Passwd not req. |
[ ] Temp. duplicate | [X] Normal account | [ ] NMS account     |
[ ] Domain trust ac | [ ] Wks trust act. | [ ] Srv trust act   |
[X] Pwd don't expir | [ ] Auto lockout   | [ ] (unknown 0x08)  |
[ ] (unknown 0x10)  | [ ] (unknown 0x20) | [ ] (unknown 0x40)  |

Failed login count: 0, while max tries is: 0
Total  login count: 485

- - - - User Edit Menu:
 1 - Clear (blank) user password
(2 - Unlock and enable user account) [seems unlocked already]
 3 - Promote user (make user an administrator)
 4 - Add user to a group
 5 - Remove user from a group
 q - Quit editing user, back to user select
Select: [q] >
```

7) After you clear the password, you should see the message "Password cleared!" The User Edit menu will be displayed again, so the message will appear at the top. Press q (quit editing user) and then Enter.

```
Password cleared!
================= USER EDIT =================
RID      : 1000 [03e8]
Username: mikey
fullname:
comment :
homedir :

00000220 = Administrators (which has 2 members)

Account bits: 0x0214 =
[ ] Disabled        | [ ] Homedir req.   | [X] Passwd not req. |
[ ] Temp. duplicate | [X] Normal account | [ ] NMS account     |
[ ] Domain trust ac | [ ] Wks trust act. | [ ] Srv trust act   |
[X] Pwd don't expir | [ ] Auto lockout   | [ ] (unknown 0x08)  |
[ ] (unknown 0x10)  | [ ] (unknown 0x20) | [ ] (unknown 0x40)  |

Failed login count: 0, while max tries is: 0
Total  login count: 485

- - - - User Edit Menu:
 1 - Clear (blank) user password
(2 - Unlock and enable user account) [seems unlocked already]
 3 - Promote user (make user an administrator)
 4 - Add user to a group
 5 - Remove user from a group
 q - Quit editing user, back to user select
Select: [q] >
```

8) At the chntpw Main Interactive Menu, press q to quit and then Enter.

```
======== chntpw Main Interactive Menu ========

Loaded hives: <SAM>

  1 - Edit user data and passwords
  2 - List groups
    - - -
  9 - Registry editor, now with full write support!
  q - Quit (you will be asked if there is something to save)

What to do? [1] ->
```

9) You should see a message indicating that the SAM hive has changed. Press y and Enter.

```
Hives that have changed:
 #   Name
 0   <SAM> - OK

==========================================================
¤ Step FOUR: Writing back changes
==========================================================
About to write file(s) back! Do it? [n] :
```

10) A message should be displayed indicating that the task completed. Press Enter to accept the default of no at the New run prompt.

```
Writing SAM

***** EDIT COMPLETE *****

You can try again if it somehow failed, or you selected wrong
New run? [n] :
```

11) You are now done and it is time to remove the ISO image and reboot the VMware machine.

```
==========================================================

* end of scripts.. returning to the shell..
* Press CTRL-ALT-DEL to reboot now (remove floppy first)
* or do whatever you want from the shell..
* However, if you mount something, remember to umount before reboot
* You may also restart the script procedure with 'sh /scripts/main.sh'
```

Remove the ISO image

To remove the ISO image from the virtual CD/DVD drive, press the Ctrl+Alt keys to release the mouse from the VMware machine window.

Select VM, Settings and then select CD/DVD, "Use physical drive." Click OK

Reboot the VMware machine

Select VM, Power, Restart Guest

Step 7: Installing VMware Tools

To add features to the VMware machine, such as improved mouse and video performance, you will want to install VMware Tools. This install package is on an ISO image and is part of VMware Workstation. It is the equivalent to installing the motherboard drivers on a new computer system. The computer may run with standard drivers, but it will run better with the correct drivers.

While the machine is running and you are logged into a user account, click the VM pulldown menu and then select Install VMware Tools. This will mount the ISO image in the virtual CD/DVD drive. An autoplay window may appear. If not, open Windows Explorer and select the CD/DVD drive. Look for setup.exe (for 32-bit machines) or setup64.exe (for 64-bit machines). Run the appropriate setup file and select Typical as the setup type.

After VMware Tools completes the installation, you will be prompted to reboot the machine.

Once you login as a user, you can set the video resolution to your needs.

You may want to consider creating a new snapshot at this point so you can return to this point if necessary. Your last snapshot was the baseline you created at the beginning of this process.

Running VMware In The Future

If you need to run this VMware machine in the future, you will need to mount the evidence file again using FTK Imager. You may only need to set the mount type to Physical disk if you do not have a need for your host computer to connect to the write-blocked logical partitions.

If the physical drive number does not match the original drive number, then you will need to edit the Mounted E01.vmdk file to reflect the new drive number. Once the physical drive number is correct, you should be able to boot the VMware machine.

Appendix C:
Timeline Analysis

This section is designed as a classroom exercise to walk you through a simple demonstration of the benefits of timeline analysis. This section includes information on how to setup and use the SANS Investigative Forensic Toolkit (SIFT) Workstation, mount an evidence file, and create a Super Timeline using log2timeline.

Getting Started

This section will walk you through the process of using the SIFT Workstation to build a Super Timeline from a hard drive imaged using the EnCase evidence file format (also referred to as the Expert Witness Format).

If you are interested in seeing what can be done with timeline analysis without going through the process yourself, jump ahead to the Case Study section.

First you will need to download the SIFT Workstation from the SANS Institute (www.sans.org). At this time of this writing, SANS is distributing version 2.14 of the SIFT Workstation. You will need to create an account to download the file. While you are there, you may want to bookmark the site as it is full of great resources geared towards forensic examiners. As a side note, if you are ever offered the opportunity to attend one of their classes, take it as their classes are excellent.

You will need to install either VMware Workstation or Player, which is the free version, on your computer. To download VMware Player, visit www.vmware.com and select Downloads. If you're on a tight budget, your total investment in the SIFT Workstation and VMware Player will be $0 (except your time, of course).

Once you have the VMware software installed, unzip the SIFT Workstation download. Start VMware and select Open a Virtual Machine. Navigate to the folder containing the SIFT Workstation, select the SIFT Workstation vmx file, and click Open.

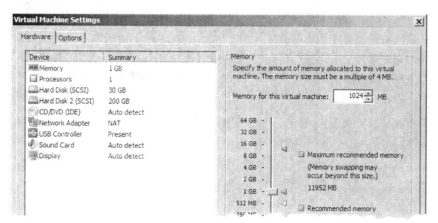

Before you get started, you will want to edit the virtual machine settings. One of the first settings you will want to change is the memory. Currently the SIFT Workstation is running a 32-bit version of the Ubuntu operating system so the maximum amount of RAM it can use is 3 GB. However, there is a modification that you can apply once it is up and running to use more RAM. While I would wait until you feel that you need more than 3 GB of RAM to do your work, the procedures for this modification can be found at the following URL:

www.ubuntugeek.com/how-to-use-more-than-3gb-ram-on-32-bit-ubuntu.html

The next edit will be the number of processors. On a portable desktop computer that has 8 logical processors, I assigned 4 processors to the VMware machine.

Click on the Options tab to make one last modification.

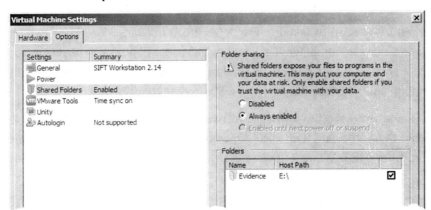

Select Shared Folders and change it to Always enabled. Modify the existing entry by highlighting it and clicking the Properties button. Set the Name field to Evidence and the Host path field to the drive and directory that contains your EnCase evidence files. Click OK to close the Properties window and click OK to close the Settings window.

As a simple precaution, make sure the evidence files on your hard drive have the read-only attribute set. I *assume* you are working with a copy of the evidence files, but there is no need to create extra work if something goes wrong.

Start the SIFT Workstation by clicking on the Play virtual machine button. As it starts, you may see a notice a dialog box prompting you to download VMware Tools

for Linux. You can download it, however, you will not need the update for this machine at this time.

Once the workstation finishes the boot process, you will be presented with a login prompt. Click sanforensics and the password is *forensics*.

First Steps

The first thing you will need to do before you can mount your image is elevate your login privilege to superuser. In the terminal window, type: sudo su

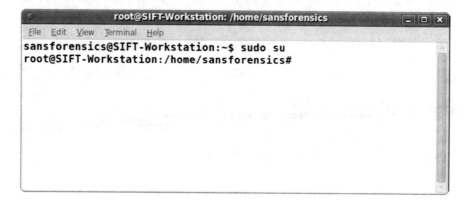

The terminal window now shows you are the root user and you are in the /home/sanforensics directory.

On the Desktop, you will see a shortcut icon called VMware-Shared-Drive.

Double-click that icon and make sure you can see the Evidence folder icon. This is the Shared Folder you created earlier in the Virtual Machine Settings. Double-click on that icon and you should see your evidence files. If you need to make a change, click on the Player pulldown menu and select Manage, Virtual Machine Settings.

Mounting Your Evidence

To mount your evidence, you are going to use the terminal window and the mount_ewf.py command. The syntax for this command is:

mount_ewf.py [image_name].E01 [mount_point]

As you start to type the command, use the auto-complete function by clicking the [TAB] key. For example, type mount_ and then click the [TAB] key. This will finish the command by adding ewf.py. This function is helpful to ensure that you syntax is correct when it comes to a filename or path. After the mount_ewf.py command, type the following and use the [TAB] key to help as you type:

./Desktop/VMware-Shared-Drive/Evidence/[image_name].E01 /mnt/ewf

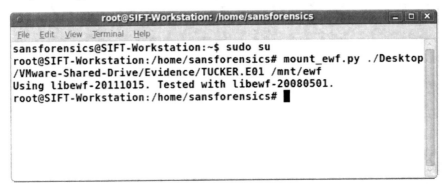

```
root@SIFT-Workstation: /home/sansforensics

File  Edit  View  Terminal  Help
sansforensics@SIFT-Workstation:~$ sudo su
root@SIFT-Workstation:/home/sansforensics# mount_ewf.py ./Desktop
/VMware-Shared-Drive/Evidence/TUCKER.E01 /mnt/ewf
Using libewf-20111015. Tested with libewf-20080501.
root@SIFT-Workstation:/home/sansforensics# █
```

Since you were already in the /home/sanforensics directory, the syntax following the mount_ewf.py command started with a dot, which means start in this directory. Then you provide the full path to your evidence files. In this example, I mounted an evidence file called TUCKER.E01. At the end, you add the mount point (/mnt/ewf), which had already been created for you.

Check the mount point by using the change directory command: cd /mnt/ewf. Use the list directory command with the switch to list all the files in long format: ls -l.

```
┌─ root@SIFT-Workstation: /mnt/ewf ─────────────── _ □ x ─┐
│ File  Edit  View  Terminal  Help                        │
│ sansforensics@SIFT-Workstation:~$ sudo su               │
│ root@SIFT-Workstation:/home/sansforensics# mount_ewf.py ./Desktop │
│ /VMware-Shared-Drive/Evidence/TUCKER.E01 /mnt/ewf       │
│ Using libewf-20111015. Tested with libewf-20080501.     │
│ root@SIFT-Workstation:/home/sansforensics# cd /mnt/ewf  │
│ root@SIFT-Workstation:/mnt/ewf# ls -l                   │
│ total 62914561                                          │
│ -r--r--r-- 1 root root 64424509440 1970-01-01 00:00 TUCKER │
│ -r--r--r-- 1 root root         318 1970-01-01 00:00 TUCKER.txt │
│ root@SIFT-Workstation:/mnt/ewf#                         │
└──────────────────────────────────────────────────────────┘
```

You will see that you have two entries. The second entry, TUCKER.txt, contains the header information of the E01 file. You can display that information by typing: cat [filename].txt

```
┌─ root@SIFT-Workstation: /mnt/ewf ─────────────── _ □ x ─┐
│ File  Edit  View  Terminal  Help                        │
│ total 62914561                                          │
│ -r--r--r-- 1 root root 64424509440 1970-01-01 00:00 TUCKER │
│ -r--r--r-- 1 root root         318 1970-01-01 00:00 TUCKER.txt │
│ root@SIFT-Workstation:/mnt/ewf# cat TUCKER.txt          │
│ # Description: Craig Tucker Desktop                     │
│ # Case number: 2013-12-001                              │
│ # Examiner name: Pixley                                 │
│ # Evidence number: 001                                  │
│ # Notes: Not provided                                   │
│ # Acquiry date: 2013-12-28T20:06:47                     │
│ # System date: 2013-12-28T20:06:47                      │
│ # Operating system used: Linux                          │
│ # Software version used: 20130331                       │
│ 4e1832956d635ec4e4feba8775a83661 */mnt/ewf/TUCKER       │
│ root@SIFT-Workstation:/mnt/ewf# █                       │
└──────────────────────────────────────────────────────────┘
```

The first entry, TUCKER (no extension), is the actual block data. As you can see in this example, the data is about 60 GB in size. However, this data is not mounted for review and needs to be mounted into a readable directory structure.

Running Log2timeline

The tool used to create a Super Timeline is called log2timeline and it has many features and options. To keep this simple, you are going to use an automated version called log2timeline-sift. This is a pre-configured version that will extract time stamps from several locations. Since I will be using a hard drive image of a Windows 7

computer, I will be using the option -win7. This option tells the tool to pull time stamps from the following locations:

Name	Description
evtx	Windows Event Log File (EVTX)
exif	Extract metadata information from files using ExifTool
ff_bookmark	Firefox bookmark file
firefox2	Firefox 2 browser history
firefox3	Firefox 3 history file
iehistory	Index.dat file containg IE history
iis	IIS W3C log file
mcafee	Log files from McAfee AV engine
mcafeefireup	XeXAMInventory or AeXProcessList log file
mcafeehel	McAfee HIPS event.log file
mcafeehs	McAfee HIPShield log file
mft	NTFS MFT file
ntuser	NTUSER.DAT registry file
openvpn	openVPN log file
opera	Opera's global history file
oxml	OpenXML document (Office 2007 documents)
pdf	PDF document metadata
prefetch	Prefetch directory
recycler	Recycle bin directory
restore	Restore point directory
safari	Safari History.plist file
sam	SAM registry file
security	SECURITY registry file
skype_sql	Skype database
software	SOFTWARE registry file
sol	.sol (LSO) or a Flash cookie file
symantec	Symantec log file
system	SYSTEM registry file
win_link	Windows shortcut file (or a link file)
wmiprov	wmiprov log file
xpfirewall	XP Firewall log

In this example, the computer was set to Pacific time so you need to make sure that all of the output is in Pacific time. As log2timeline goes through the data, it will find time stamps that are stored in UTC time and some that are stored in local time. You need to specify the time zone so all of the time stamps are normalized into one setting, which is an important step for conducting timeline analysis.

The syntax for this version of log2timeline is as follows:

log2timeline-sift -win7 -z PST8PDT -i [image]

In this case, I used the option -win7 as this was a Windows 7 computer (as opposed to Windows XP).

```
root@SIFT-Workstation: /mnt/ewf
File  Edit  View  Terminal  Help
sansforensics@SIFT-Workstation:~$ sudo su
root@SIFT-Workstation:/home/sansforensics# mount_ewf.py ./Desktop
/VMware-Shared-Drive/Evidence/TUCKER.E01 /mnt/ewf
Using libewf-20111015. Tested with libewf-20080501.
root@SIFT-Workstation:/home/sansforensics# cd /mnt/ewf
root@SIFT-Workstation:/mnt/ewf# ls -l
total 62914561
-r--r--r-- 1 root root 64424509440 1970-01-01 00:00 TUCKER
-r--r--r-- 1 root root         318 1970-01-01 00:00 TUCKER.txt
root@SIFT-Workstation:/mnt/ewf# log2timeline-sift -win7 -z PST8PD
T -i TUCKER
Image file (TUCKER) has not been mounted. Do you want me to mount
 it for you? [y|n]: y
```

The tool detected that I had not mounted TUCKER to read the file system and offers to mount it for me (*Do you want me to mount it for you?*). Type y and hit [ENTER].

```
                                                         root@SIFT-Workstation: /mnt/ewf          [_] [□] [X]
 File  Edit  View  Terminal  Help
 T -i TUCKER
 Image file (TUCKER) has not been mounted. Do you want me to mount
  it for you? [y|n]: y
 No partition nr. has been provided, attempting to print it out.
 DOS Partition Table
 Offset Sector: 0
 Units are in 512-byte sectors

        Slot       Start          End            Length         Description
 00:    Meta       0000000000     0000000000     0000000001     Primary Table
   (#0)
 01:    -----      0000000000     0000002047     0000002048     Unallocated
 02:    00:00      0000002048     0125827071     0125825024     NTFS (0x07)
 03:    -----      0125827072     0125829119     0000002048     Unallocated
 Which partion would you like to mount?: [1-3]: 2
```

The tool then runs the mmls (media management list) command from the Sleuth Kit, which is incorporated into the workstation, to display the partition table of the image. In my example, partition 2 is the partition that contains the operating system I want to analyze, so press 2 and hit [ENTER].

At that point, log2timeline starts pulling time stamps. This process can take a couple of hours so go find something else to do for a while. Although you may not see any scrolling text in the terminal window for a while, do not assume it stopped working. Look at the system monitor icon in the bottom right pane and you will see active processor activity.

Bodyfile and Filtering

Once the tool is finished, you will have an output file that is referred to as a "bodyfile." You can locate this file by clicking on the cases shortcut icon on the Desktop. Inside that directory is a directory called timeline-output-folder and it will contain the bodyfile called [image_name]_bodyfile.txt. This file can easily contain over one million entries, including duplicate information, and it needs to be filtered.

In order to filter the bodyfile, you are going to use another tool called l2t_process. This tool will remove duplicate entries and combine entries from the MFT that have the same time stamp. For example, a new file may have the same created and last accessed time. Instead of listing these entries twice, they are combined into one entry.

Another helpful feature of l2t_process is the ability to whitelist entries. For example, you may want to exclude Internet cache file entries from your timeline. To do this, use the File Browser and open the cases/timeline-output-folder directory.

Select File, Create Document, Empty File. Name the file whitelist.txt. Double-click on the file, which will open it with a text editor called gedit.

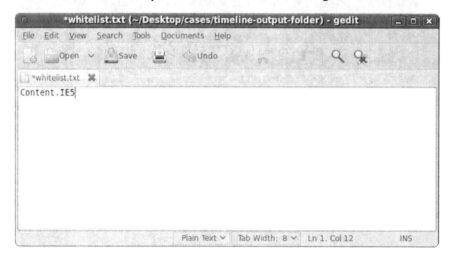

Each word you want to exclude needs to be on a separate line. Type Content.IE5 and then click Save. Do not hit [Enter] after Content.IE5 unless you want to add a second word. You do not want to create a null entry as a whitelisted word.

Using the terminal window, change directory to the timeline-output-folder directory:

cd /home/sanforensics/Desktop/cases/timeline-output-folder

```
root@SIFT-Workstation: /home/sansforensics/Desktop/cases/timeline-outpu  _  □  x
File  Edit  View  Terminal  Help
Wide character in print at /usr/bin/log2timeline-sift line 400.
Wide character in print at /usr/bin/log2timeline-sift line 400.
Wide character in print at /usr/bin/log2timeline-sift line 400.
Wide character in print at /usr/bin/log2timeline-sift line 400.
Wide character in print at /usr/bin/log2timeline-sift line 400.
Wide character in print at /usr/bin/log2timeline-sift line 400.
Wide character in print at /usr/bin/log2timeline-sift line 400.
Wide character in print at /usr/bin/log2timeline-sift line 400.
Wide character in print at /usr/bin/log2timeline-sift line 400.
umount: /mnt/windows_mount: device is busy.
        (In some cases useful info about processes that use
        the device is found by lsof(8) or fuser(1))
root@SIFT-Workstation:/mnt/ewf# cd /home/sansforensics/Desktop/ca
ses/timeline-output-folder/
root@SIFT-Workstation:/home/sansforensics/Desktop/cases/timeline-
output-folder#
```

There are different options available to use with l2t_process. You can even filter the data by a specific date range. The syntax you are going to use in this example is:

l2t_process -b [bodyfile] -w [whitelist] [date_range] > timeline.csv

In this example, the output is based on a date range of 12-17-2013 to present and the output is going to a new file called timeline.csv.

```
root@SIFT-Workstation: /home/sansforensics/Desktop/cases/timeline-outpu _ □ ×
File  Edit  View  Terminal  Help
root@SIFT-Workstation:/home/sansforensics/Desktop/cases/timeline-
output-folder# l2t_process -b TUCKER_bodyfile.txt -w whitelist.tx
t 12-17-2013 > timeline.csv
Building whitelist (known good)...DONE (1 keywords loaded)
There are 25 that fall outside the scope of the date range, yet s
how sign of possible timestomping.
Would you like to include them in the output? [Y/n]

Total number of events that fit into the filter (got printed) = 1
30282
Total number of duplicate entries removed = 13856
Total number of events skipped due to whitelisting = 0
Total number of events skipped due to keyword filtering = 0
Total number of processed entries = 623493
Run time of the tool: 44 sec
root@SIFT-Workstation:/home/sansforensics/Desktop/cases/timeline-
output-folder# ▋
```

During the processing, the tool incorporated the whitelist, which contained one keyword. The process also discovered some possible entries of "timestomping," which means that someone may have intentionally altered time stamps. This can produce some false positives so do not assume this means that someone had altered the time stamps. As you can see, the filtering process took the total number of entries of 623,493 down to a more manageable list of 130,282.

Formatting the Timeline

On the SANS website, you can find an Excel template to color-code the timeline. This template is associated with their blog page dated January 25, 2012. The blog page provides a link for the download along with the instructions to import your timeline into the template.

Case Study

In this case study, a person is suspected of downloading child pornography during chat sessions using Windows Live Messenger.

There were multiple files found in the user's My Received Files folder. A partial listing of those files below shows files that were created on 5/23/2010:

Date	Time (Pacific)	Filename
5/23/10	22:59:40	09.jpg
5/23/10	23:05:05	08.jpg
5/23/10	23:09:32	012.jpg
5/23/10	23:17:05	011.jpg
5/23/10	23:45:32	014.jpg
5/23/10	23:45:39	013.jpg
5/23/10	23:45:45	015.jpg

Starting on 5/23/2010, at 22:59, look at the timeline in Excel to see what other activity was occurring before and after that time.

By using Excel, you will be able to quickly navigate through the timeline by using the filter. Start by filtering the date column to May 23, 2010.

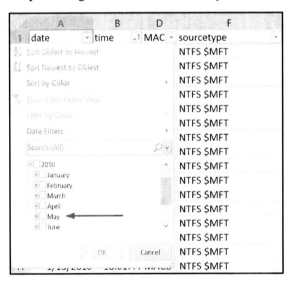

Once you have date filtered, scroll down until you see the first file at 22:59.

MACB

In column D, you will notice that the heading is labeled MACB. This column identifies the timestamps in MACtime format. Since the file system is NTFS, these abbreviations are defined as follows:

> M = modified
> A = accessed
> C = MFT record change
> B = born (file created time)

This type of abbreviation can be a little confusing as you may have been taught that the C means created. If you are looking for created, then look for B (born), as C means change.

date	time	MACB	sourcetype	desc
5/23/2010	22:11:11	...B	NTFS $MFT	/$Recycle.Bin/$-1-5-21-1994735003-1233277250-1681396048-1000/$RPYLQUJ
5/23/2010	22:13:43	...B	NTFS $MFT	/$Recycle.Bin/$-1-5-21-1994735003-1233277250-1681396048-1000/$RPYLQUJ/New folder1/New
5/23/2010	22:38:50	.A.B	NTFS $MFT	/Users/Owner/AppData/Local/Microsoft/Windows Live Mail/Hotmail (de 4a6/Sent items/000294823
5/23/2010	22:38:51	M.C.	NTFS $MFT	/Users/Owner/AppData/Local/Microsoft/Windows Live Mail/Hotmail (de 4a6/Sent items/000294823
5/23/2010	22:39:34	.A.B	NTFS $MFT	/Users/Owner/AppData/Local/Microsoft/Windows Live Mail/Hotmail (de 4a6/Sent items/000294823
5/23/2010	22:39:35	M.C.	NTFS $MFT	/Users/Owner/AppData/Local/Microsoft/Windows Live Mail/Hotmail (de 4a6/Sent items/000294823
5/23/2010	22:41:07	MACB	NTFS $MFT	/Users/Owner/AppData/Local/Microsoft/Windows Live Mail/Hotmail (de 4a6/Sent items/000294823
5/23/2010	22:56:29	M.C.	NTFS $MFT	/Users/Owner/AppData/Local/Google/Toolbar History/thumbnails/00000047.png
5/23/2010	22:56:29	M.C.	NTFS $MFT	/Users/Owner/AppData/Local/Google/Toolbar History/urls/00000047
5/23/2010	22:56:35	MACB	Internet Explorer	URL:https://online.wellsfargo.com/das/cgi-bin2/session.cgi?sessargs=D99SVN-v5kB-05omQ1nkNpo
5/23/2010	22:56:48	MACB	Internet Explorer	URL:https://online.wellsfargo.com/das/cgi-bin/session.cgi?sessargs=vgeD0NRmHajXtqyC27g2Hlww
5/23/2010	22:56:55	MACB	Internet Explorer	URL:https://online.wellsfargo.com/das/cgi-bin/session.cgi?sessargs=YW0b9oZtazE_jzX4wQ4bNsGIN
5/23/2010	22:57:52	MACB	Internet Explorer	URL:http://apps.facebook.com/socialcity/?track=bookmark-20100402-1-105343&ref=bookmarks
5/23/2010	22:59:40	...B	NTFS $MFT	/Users/Owner/Documents/My Received Files/09.jpg
5/23/2010	22:59:41	A...	NTFS $MFT	/Users/Owner/Documents/My Received Files/09.jpg
5/23/2010	22:59:42	M...	NTFS $MFT	/Users/Owner/Documents/My Received Files/09.jpg
5/23/2010	23:05:05	...B	NTFS $MFT	/Users/Owner/Documents/My Received Files/08.jpg
5/23/2010	23:05:12	A...	NTFS $MFT	/Users/Owner/Documents/My Received Files/08.jpg
5/23/2010	23:09:32	...B	NTFS $MFT	/Users/Owner/Documents/My Received Files/012.jpg
5/23/2010	23:09:33	MA...	NTFS $MFT	/Users/Owner/Documents/My Received Files/012.jpg
5/23/2010	23:17:05	...B	NTFS $MFT	/Users/Owner/Documents/My Received Files/011.jpg
5/23/2010	23:17:05	MACB	NTFS $MFT	/Users/Owner/AppData/Roaming/Microsoft/Windows/Recent/011.lnk
5/23/2010	23:17:06	A...	NTFS $MFT	/Users/Owner/Documents/My Received Files/011.jpg
5/23/2010	23:17:07	M	NTFS $MFT	/Users/Owner/Documents/My Received Files/011.jpg

If you look at the activity prior to the files being stored in the My Received Files folder, you will notice that there is Internet Explorer activity with Wells Fargo's website. Could the person behind the keyboard be logged into his online banking account?

Prior to that activity, you see file activity associated with Windows Live Mail. This prompts you to take a look at email activity. In this case, the user configured Live Mail to send and receive email from a Hotmail account.

Date	Time (Pacific)	Path	Subject
5/23/10	22:38:48	Sent	Apartment manager (Balboa, CA)
5/23/10	22:39:32	Sent	attention Maria
5/23/10	22:41:05	Sent	Resident managers resume (china town)
5/23/10	23:37:31	Sent	Apartment manager (west los angeles)
5/23/10	23:56:17	Sent	Janitorial manager resume (glendale)

While these files were being created, someone was sending email from Windows Live Mail. You check the emails and find that they contain the defendant's resumes and he was actively seeking employment.

Your analysis of the timeline has been helpful so far. Now let's move to the next day in question.

The next day that involved files being created in the My Received Files folder was on 6/22/2010.

Date	Time (Pacific)	Filename
6/22/10	19:17:34	12062.jpg
6/22/10	19:20:50	20091217215303-nzrtxzidmzfcvfwgg.jpg
6/22/10	19:23:24	20100127125605-fcvekydvzcqvvvqwz.jpg
6/22/10	19:23:36	20090311021804-bntgfezxrsuhyktol.jpg
6/22/10	19:26:00	20100129093947-fcvekydvzcqvvvqwz.jpg
6/22/10	19:29:02	20100521075912-fmypvvxkxpqagxkjv.jpg
6/22/10	19:31:26	20100129133148-fcvekydvzcqvvvqwz.jpg
6/22/10	19:54:32	8F[1].JPG
6/22/10	19:54:40	!14yobone(1).jpg
6/22/10	19:57:34	AD.jpg
6/22/10	20:01:16	389264155_IPFRFGYUKJTWMGE.jpg
6/22/10	20:04:59	6u.jpg
6/22/10	20:05:05	ASD.jpg
6/22/10	20:05:34	ASDF.jpg
6/22/10	20:07:41	ASDFDT.jpg
6/22/10	20:11:14	!!SWEE~1.mpeg
6/22/10	20:19:14	mnbb_chunk_3.wmv
6/22/10	20:31:58	NI_0030.wmv

Filter your timeline to June 22, 2010 and scroll down until you see the first file at 19:17.

About 20 minutes prior to this first file being created, you notice more file activity associated with Windows Live Mail.

date	time	MACB	sourcetype	desc
6/22/2010	18:56:33	A..B	NTFS $MFT	/Users/Owner/AppData/Local/Microsoft/Windows Live Mail/Hotmail (de 4a6/Sent items/00294823
6/22/2010	18:56:34	M.C.	NTFS $MFT	/Users/Owner/AppData/Local/Microsoft/Windows Live Mail/Hotmail (de 4a6/Sent items/00294823
6/22/2010	19:05:35	...B	NTFS $MFT	/Users/Owner/AppData/Local/Temp/Low/Cookies/owner@livefilestore[2].txt
6/22/2010	19:06:24	ACB	Internet Explorer	URL:aptm.phoenix.edu/
6/22/2010	19:09:25	MAC.	NTFS $MFT	/Users/Owner/AppData/Roaming/Microsoft/Windows/SendTo
6/22/2010	19:17:34	A..B	NTFS $MFT	/Users/Owner/Documents/My Received Files/12062.jpg
6/22/2010	19:17:45	M.C.	NTFS $MFT	/Users/Owner/Documents/My Received Files/12062.jpg
6/22/2010	19:20:50	A..B	NTFS $MFT	/Users/Owner/Documents/My Received Files/20091217215303-nzrtxzidmzfcvfwgg.jpg
6/22/2010	19:20:57	M.C.	NTFS $MFT	/Users/Owner/Documents/My Received Files/20091217215303-nzrtxzidmzfcvfwgg.jpg
6/22/2010	19:23:24	...B	NTFS $MFT	/Users/Owner/Documents/My Received Files/20100127125605-fcvekydvzcqvvvqwz.jpg
6/22/2010	19:23:25	A...	NTFS $MFT	/Users/Owner/Documents/My Received Files/20100127125605-fcvekydvzcqvvvqwz.jpg
6/22/2010	19:23:27	M.C.	NTFS $MFT	/Users/Owner/Documents/My Received Files/20100127125605-fcvekydvzcqvvvqwz.jpg
6/22/2010	19:23:36	A..B	NTFS $MFT	/Users/Owner/Documents/My Received Files/20090311021804-bntgfezxrsuhyktoi.jpg
6/22/2010	19:23:49	M.C.	NTFS $MFT	/Users/Owner/Documents/My Received Files/20090311021804-bntgfezxrsuhyktoi.jpg
6/22/2010	19:26:00	A..B	NTFS $MFT	/Users/Owner/Documents/My Received Files/20100129093947-fcvekydvzcqvvvqwz.jpg
6/22/2010	19:27:03	M...	NTFS $MFT	/Users/Owner/Documents/My Received Files/20100129093947-fcvekydvzcqvvvqwz.jpg
6/22/2010	19:27:04	..C.	NTFS $MFT	/Users/Owner/Documents/My Received Files/20100129093947-fcvekydvzcqvvvqwz.jpg
6/22/2010	19:29:02	A..B	NTFS $MFT	/Users/Owner/Documents/My Received Files/20100521075912-fmypvvxkxpqagxkiv.jpg
6/22/2010	19:29:24	M.C.	NTFS $MFT	/Users/Owner/Documents/My Received Files/20100521075912-fmypvvxkxpqagxkiv.jpg
6/22/2010	19:31:26	A..B	NTFS $MFT	/Users/Owner/Documents/My Received Files/20100129133148-fcvekydvzcqvvvqwz.jpg
6/22/2010	19:31:42	M...	NTFS $MFT	/Users/Owner/Documents/My Received Files/20100129133148-fcvekydvzcqvvvqwz.jpg
6/22/2010	19:31:43	..C.	NTFS $MFT	/Users/Owner/Documents/My Received Files/20100129133148-fcvekydvzcqvvvqwz.jpg
6/22/2010	19:47:28	MACB	NTUSER key	Key name: HKEY_USER/Software/Microsoft/Windows/CurrentVersion/Explorer/ComDlg32/OpenSa
6/22/2010	19:48:12	MACB	NTUSER key	Key name: HKEY_USER/Software/Microsoft/WindowsLive/CommunicationsClients/Shared/1593827

Date	Time (Pacific)	Path	Subject
6/22/10	17:43:22	Sent	Loss prevention agent resume
6/22/10	18:56:30	Sent	Property management resume
6/22/10	21:24:49	Sent	Security officer resume

A quick review of the email activity stored in Windows Live Mail shows the defendant was seeking employment again and sending out his resume.

While not all timeline analysis may be this easy, it can certainly help provide a high-level overview of what is going on with the computer at a specific date and time. It is certainly worth a look.

Appendix D:
Demonstrative Kiosk

This section provides a simple method that can be used as a demonstrative exhibit to project a user's computer environment during a trial.

Trial Presentation

In Chapter 2, I mentioned that you could use screenshots of the user login screen and the desktop as a simple way to describe the user's basic computer environment. In one trial, counsel wanted to expand on that concept by using a live demonstration of the user's computer during trial. Opposing counsel objected as it was not guaranteed that the environment could be controlled and information that was not submitted in discovery could inadvertently be disclosed during a live demonstration.

The question posed by counsel was could the user's environment be demonstrated in a way that would be canned for discovery purposes, but also appear to be live. During direct, the demonstrative exhibit would be used to display the user's files and other findings, such as the user's recently played movies.

The solution was a PowerPoint presentation that performed in a kiosk mode. The presentation ended up consisting of 47 slides with hyperlinks, which appeared as icons in each slide. When clicked, the hyperlinks would cause the presentation to jump to specific slides within the presentation and also allow a reverse direction. This presentation was easily produced in discovery since it basically consisted of 47 printed pages. While it may seem complicated, it was a fairly easy presentation to build.

The opening screenshot consisted of the user's desktop (Figure 5-1). In this particular slide, there were three hyperlinks that appeared to be normal icons within the screenshot (**Note**: The circles around each hyperlink were added only to demonstrate their positioning and are not visible in the actual slides).

Figure 5-1 - PowerPoint slide with hyperlinks

The first hyperlink was the Macintosh HD icon, which launched a different slide that displayed the contents of that specific folder. The Apple icon in the top left corner was a hyperlink that opened the Apple pulldown menu. The tab icon in the lower left screen appeared in each slide and was a hyperlink that would bring the presentation back to the first slide.

Figure 5-2 displayed the contents of the Macintosh HD folder with one hyperlink set to open the Documents folder. The other hyperlink was the square icon in the top left corner of the window and was configured to close the window.

Figure 5-2 - Contents of folder

In Figure 5-3, the recently accessed files (which have been redacted) were listed in the pop-out box. There are two hyperlinks outlined: one to open RealPlayer (Figure 5-4) and the other to open Windows Media Player.

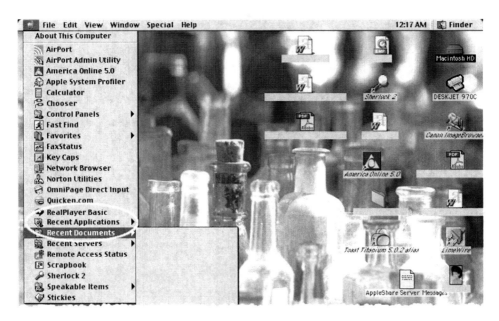

Figure 5-3 - Demonstration of recent documents (redacted)

Figure 5-4 - RealPlayer listing the recently played files (redacted)

In Figure 5-5, the jury could see the user-created "z folder" that the user moved the illegal images and videos into after downloading them using LimeWire. Hyperlinks were added to the up and down arrows located in the lower right portion of the window. These hyperlinks would scroll the window up and down in an effort to demonstrate all of the files within the folder.

Figure 5-5 - Demonstration of the user-created folder that contained the illegal images and videos

Appendix E:
Sample Questions

This section contains categories of questions and sample questions that may be used during the interview process. These questions are meant to be a simple guide to provide some direction. The person conducting the interview should try to ask open ended questions to elicit responses beyond yes and no, such as "Tell me about your background with computers."

Ownership

Is this your computer?

> Do you know the speed of the processor?

> Do you know the size of the hard drive?

Was the computer given to you or did you buy it?

> When did you buy it?

> Where did you buy it?

> How much did you pay for it?

How many computers do you own?

Who else uses this computer?

How often do you use this computer?

Background

Tell me about your background with computers.

How many computers have you owned?

What happened to your old computers?

Have you ever had to replace a hard drive or upgrade a part, like a video card?

> Did you do it or have someone else do it?

How did you transfer your data from one hard drive to another?

Have you ever built you own computer?

> Tell me about that.

What kind of devices do you have connected to your computer?

How would you describe yourself as a computer user? (beginner, average, or advanced)

Do you own any computer books?

> Which books do you own?

What computer subjects have you studied?

Was this through a class at school or something you did on your own?

Operating Systems

What operating system is currently installed on your computer?

What operating systems are you familiar with?

Have you ever installed or upgraded an operating system?

Tell me about the process you went through to [install or upgrade].

User Accounts

Are you the only user of this computer?

Do you have a password to log in?

What is your password?

Do other people know your password?

Does anyone else log in to your account?

How many people use this computer?

What are their names?

How can I contact them?

Do they use your user account or a separate user account?

What other accounts are set up on the computer?

Does each account have a different password?

Did you setup the accounts and passwords?

Do you know the passwords of the other accounts?

How do you keep your data from other users on the computer?

Do you try to hide your data from other users?

How do you do that?

Passwords

What programs do you use that require passwords?

Describe your passwords. Do they incorporate letters, numbers, special characters, spaces or capitalization?

What are all of the passwords you use?

What do you use these passwords for?

Who else knows your passwords?

Installed Programs

What software (programs) do you primarily use on your computer?

Did you install the software or is this software that was pre-installed?

What software have you purchased?

Is this software registered in your name or someone else?

Do you use any software to clean your activity from the computer, such as Internet history or opening files?

What software do you use?

Have you ever had someone install files or programs on your computer without your permission?

What was installed?

When did this happen?

How did the person get access to do this?

File Deletion

How often do you empty the Recycle Bin?

Do you use any software to wipe your data?

What software do you use?

Why do you use this software?

What prompted you to start using this software?

Personal Files

What types of personal files do you store on the computer?

Does anyone else have access to your personal files?

> Who has access?

> How can I contact them?

Digital Photos and Movies

What types of digital photos or movies do you have stored on the computer?

How do you organize your these files?

> Do you organize the files by age or something else?

Encryption

Do you use any kind of encryption?

> Tell me about how you setup the encryption.

> What software do you use?

> Have you encrypted the entire drive?

> Have you created any encrypted containers?

>> Where are they stored?

> Have you created any hidden encrypted containers?

> Do you use a password or a passphrase?

>> What is it?

> Do you also use a key file in addition to your [password or passphrase]?

Backup

Do you backup your data?

> How do you backup your data?

> Where do you keep your backup data?

Do you use an online backup service?

Which service do you use?

How long have you used this service?

Do you use CD's or DVD's to burn or copy data?

Where are these discs?

External Devices

Do you own any external drives or thumb drives?

Where are they?

How long have you had these devices?

Are these your devices or have some of them been given to you?

Do any of the drives use encryption?

Was the encryption pre-installed with the device or does it use another program?

What program is used with the drive?

What password, passphrase, and/or key file is used to encrypt the drive?

Compressed Files

Have you ever used a program to compress your files into a single file?

What program do you use?

Do you protect the files with a password?

What is your password?

People have different reasons for needing to compress files like this, why do you do it?

Network and Internet Service

Is this computer part of a network in your [home, business]?

Who maintains the network?

Where is the router?

How many computers are part of this network?

Who is your Internet service provider?

How long have you been a customer?

What kind of Internet connection do you have?

Do you use any other Internet service providers?

Do you have a wireless router?

Which computers or devices connect to the wireless signal?

Is your wireless connection open to the public?

What is the name (SSID) of your wireless signal?

How did you secure your wireless signal?

Did you give access to other people to use your wireless signal?

Who has access?

How can I contact them?

Do you have cellular broadband service?

What devices do you use to connect to this service (aircard, USB device, hotspot device)?

Who is the service provider for the device?

Internet Browser

Which Internet browser do you primarily use?

What other browsers do you use?

Do you ever use private browsing mode?

Why do you use private browsing?

How often do you clear your Internet history?

Do you clear it or is it set to clear after a certain time?

Internet Search Engines

What search engines do you use on a regular basis?

What types of things do you search for?

Email

Do you use email?

What email accounts do you use?

How do you access your email? (Web interface, software, mobile device)

How long have you used these accounts?

How many people are listed in your email address book?

How do you know these people?

Do you use email to send and receive files?

What types of files have you sent to people?

What types of files have you received?

Does anyone else have access to your email?

Peer-to-Peer Software

What peer-to-peer programs do you use?

When did you first install the software?

Did you ever upgrade the software?

Have you uninstalled any peer-to-peer software?

Do you buy a license or do you use the free version?

Did you know how to change the settings?

What settings have you changed?

Where do you store the files that are downloaded?

What do you do with a file once it has been downloaded?

Do you copy or move the files to another folder or another drive?

How many files do you share?

Did you disable file sharing?

> When did you disable sharing?

What types of files do you search for?

What time of day do you normally search for files?

What search terms have you used?

Do you ever preview the files while they are being downloaded?

Have you ever downloaded files that you did not intend to download?

> Tell me about that.

Chat Programs

Do you chat with other people online?

> What screen names do you use?

> Which chat software do you use?

> Do you have to type in your password when you start the software?

> Are you the only person who uses this screen name?

>> Who else uses this screen name?

>> How can I contact them?

> Do you use a webcam to video chat?

> Have you ever used voice chat?

> Do you save your chat logs?

> How long have you been chatting with others?

> How many people are in your friends list?

> Do you personally know any of these people?

> Have you ever met anyone in person that you first met online?

>> How did you arranged to meet them in person?

Do you trade (send and receive) files with the people you chat with?

How do you transfer files? Do you use the chat program or use email?

What files have you sent to other people?

What files have you received?

Where do you store the files you send and receive?

Do you use chat rooms?

What chat rooms do you go to?

Do you play any type of online games in chat rooms?

Illegal Activity

Do you have any files stored on this computer that are illegal to possess?

Describe the files to me.

What makes you believe the files are illegal?

What folders are these files stored in?

Do you know how these files ended up on the computer?

Is there any justifiable reason for these files to be stored on the computer?

Do you have any files stored on this computer that you feel are inappropriate?

Please describe the files.

What makes you believe the files are inappropriate?

Online Activity

What type of online accounts do you have, such as iTunes, Netflix, or banking?

Do you play any type of online games?

What games do you play?

Do you personally know anyone you play with online?

Have you ever met anyone in person that you first met online?

What is your online profile name?

How do you pay for this account?

When are you normally online?

Have you ever used a proxy server or other type of anonymizing service?

What service did you use?

Tell me how you use this service.

Have you ever uploaded files to any online groups or file sharing sites?

What groups do you belong to?

Have you ever downloaded or uploaded any files to news groups?

What news server do you access?

How do you access the news server?

What news groups do you look at?

Social Media

Do you have a Facebook or other type of social media account, such as MySpace?

What is the name of your account?

When did you create the account?

How often do you access your account?

Does anyone else have access to your account?

How many friends do you have linked to this account?

Is your profile public or private?

Do you maintain any blog sites?

What site(s)?

How often do you access the site(s)?

Online Cloud Storage

Do you use online storage, such as Dropbox, Google Drive, or SkyDrive?

What type of data do you store online?

Virtual Computer

Do you use software to run virtual environments, such as VMware?

>What operating systems do you run?

>How do you use this environment?

>Why do you use a virtual machine?

Viruses

What anti-virus software do you use?

>Do you keep the software updated?

>How long have you been using anti-virus software?

Have you ever had a virus on your computer?

>How did you get rid of it?

>How do you think you received the virus?

Do you know what a Trojan virus is?

>What is a Trojan virus?

>Have you ever had a Trojan virus on your computer?

>How did you get rid of the Trojan virus?

Do you think anyone has ever hacked into your computer?

>When did this happen?

>Tell me about it.

>Did you ever report it or tell anyone about this?

Web Cameras

Do you have any web cameras installed in your home?

>How do you access these cameras?

>Do you keep the recordings?

>>Where do you store this data?

Mobile Devices

What type of mobile devices do you own, such as a cell phone, iPad, iPod, or other tablet?

Do these devices connect to the Internet?

 Who is your service provider?

 What type of data plan do you have?

Do you use these devices to take photographs?

Do you use these devices to record video?

Do you sync these devices to your computer?

Do you sync these devices to a cloud service?

Have you ever copied files to or from your computer?

 What types of files did you copy?

Questions for other people who have access to the computer

Do you have your own user account on the computer?

 What is the name of your account?

 What is your password?

 Does anyone else know your password?

 Do you share access on the computer with anyone else?

Do other people have access to your files?

Do you know the passwords of the other account(s)?

Have you ever accessed files stored in another user account?

What types of files do you store on the computer?

Appendix F: California Law

For reference purposes, this section contains specific codes of California law that are applicable to expert witnesses.

California Evidence Code

§720 Qualification as an expert witness

(a) A person is qualified to testify as an expert if he has special knowledge, skill, experience, training, or education sufficient to qualify him as an expert on the subject to which his testimony relates. Against the objection of a party, such special knowledge, skill, experience, training, or education must be shown before the witness may testify as an expert.

(b) A witness' special knowledge, skill, experience, training, or education may be shown by any otherwise admissible evidence, including his own testimony.

§721 Cross-examination of expert witness

(a) Subject to subdivision (b), a witness testifying as an expert may be cross-examined to the same extent as any other witness and, in addition, may be fully cross-examined as to (1) his or her qualifications, (2) the subject to which his or her expert testimony relates, and (3) the matter upon which his or her opinion is based and the reasons for his or her opinion.

(b) If a witness testifying as an expert testifies in the form of an opinion, he or she may not be cross-examined in regard to the content or tenor of any scientific, technical, or professional text, treatise, journal, or similar publication unless any of the following occurs:

(1) The witness referred to, considered, or relied upon such publication in arriving at or forming his or her opinion.

(2) The publication has been admitted in evidence.

(3) The publication has been established as a reliable authority by the testimony or admission of the witness or by other expert testimony or by judicial notice.

If admitted, relevant portions of the publication may be read into evidence but may not be received as exhibits.

§801 Expert witnesses; opinion testimony

If a witness is testifying as an expert, his testimony in the form of an opinion is limited to such an opinion as is:

(a) Related to a subject that is sufficiently beyond common experience that the opinion of an expert would assist the trier of fact; and

(b) Based on matter (including his special knowledge, skill, experience, training, and education) perceived by or personally known to the witness or made known to him at or before the hearing, whether or not admissible, that is of a type that reasonably may be relied upon by an expert in forming an opinion upon the subject to which his testimony relates, unless an expert is precluded by law from using such matter as a basis for his opinion.

§802 Statement of basis of opinion

A witness testifying in the form of an opinion may state on direct examination the reasons for his opinion and the matter (including, in the case of an expert, his special knowledge, skill, experience, training, and education) upon which it is based, unless he is precluded by law from using such reasons or matter as a basis for his opinion. The court in its discretion may require that a witness before testifying in the form of an opinion be first examined concerning the matter upon which his opinion is based.

California Code of Civil Procedure

Chapter 18, Article 2

Demand for exchange of expert witness information

§2034.210

After the setting of the initial trial date for the action, any party may obtain discovery by demanding that all parties simultaneously exchange information concerning each other's expert trial witnesses to the following extent:

(a) Any party may demand a mutual and simultaneous exchange by all parties of a list containing the name and address of any natural person, including one who is a

party, whose oral or deposition testimony in the form of an expert opinion any party expects to offer in evidence at the trial.

(b) If any expert designated by a party under subdivision (a) is a party or an employee of a party, or has been retained by a party for the purpose of forming and expressing an opinion in anticipation of the litigation or in preparation for the trial of the action, the designation of that witness shall include or be accompanied by an expert witness declaration under Section 2034.260.

(c) Any party may also include a demand for the mutual and simultaneous production for inspection and copying of all discoverable reports and writings, if any, made by any expert described in subdivision (b) in the course of preparing that expert's opinion.

§2034.260

(a) All parties who have appeared in the action shall exchange information concerning expert witnesses in writing on or before the date of exchange specified in the demand. The exchange of information may occur at a meeting of the attorneys for the parties involved or by a mailing on or before the date of exchange.

(b) The exchange of expert witness information shall include either of the following:

(1) A list setting forth the name and address of any person whose expert opinion that party expects to offer in evidence at the trial.

(2) A statement that the party does not presently intend to offer the testimony of any expert witness.

(c) If any witness on the list is an expert as described in subdivision (b) of Section 2034.210, the exchange shall also include or be accompanied by an expert witness declaration signed only by the attorney for the party designating the expert, or by that party if that party has no attorney. This declaration shall be under penalty of perjury and shall contain:

(1) A brief narrative statement of the qualifications of each expert.

(2) A brief narrative statement of the general substance of the testimony that the expert is expected to give.

(3) A representation that the expert has agreed to testify at the trial.

(4) A representation that the expert will be sufficiently familiar with the pending action to submit to a meaningful oral deposition concerning the specific testimony, including any opinion and its basis, that the expert is expected to give at trial.

(5) A statement of the expert's hourly and daily fee for providing deposition testimony and for consulting with the retaining attorney.

CPSIA information can be obtained at www.ICGtesting.com
Printed in the USA
LVOW09s2344050815

448970LV00020B/883/P

9 781492 208433